ECONOMIC NORMALIZATION WITH CUBA

A Roadmap for US Policymakers

T0323965

MIX
Paper from
responsible sources
FSC® C005010

FSC
www.fsc.org

ECONOMIC NORMALIZATION WITH CUBA

A Roadmap for US Policymakers

Gary Clyde Hufbauer
and Barbara Kotschwar

Assisted by Cathleen Cimino and Julia Muir

Peterson Institute for International Economics

Washington, DC

April 2014

Gary Clyde Hufbauer, Reginald Jones Senior Fellow at the Peterson Institute for International Economics since 1992, was the Maurice Greenberg Chair and Director of Studies at the Council on Foreign Relations (1996–98), the Marcus Wallenberg Professor of International Finance Diplomacy at Georgetown University (1985–92), senior fellow at the Institute (1981–85), deputy director of the International Law Institute at Georgetown University (1979–81); deputy assistant secretary for international trade and investment policy of the US Treasury (1977–79); and director of the international tax staff at the Treasury (1974–76). Among his numerous coauthored books are *Local Content Requirements: A Global Problem* (2013), *The United States Should Establish Permanent Normal Trade Relations with Russia* (2012), *Figuring Out the Doha Round* (2010), and *Economic Sanctions Reconsidered*, 3rd edition (2007).

Barbara Kotschwar, research fellow, has been associated with the Peterson Institute for International Economics since 2007. She is also adjunct professor of Latin American studies and economics at Georgetown University. Before joining the Institute, she was chief of the Foreign Trade Information System at the Organization of American States. She has advised Latin American and Caribbean governments on trade-related issues and has worked with multilateral and regional development banks on a variety of trade and development projects. Her publications include *Understanding the Trans-Pacific Partnership* (2012) and *Reengaging Egypt: Options for US-Egypt Economic Relations* (2010).

Cathleen Cimino has been a research analyst at the Peterson Institute for International Economics since August 2012. She obtained a master's degree focused on international economics from the School of International Relations and Pacific Studies (IR/PS) at the University of California, San Diego and a bachelor's degree from Columbia University. She previously worked on development and economic security issues at the Asia Society and the Center for Strategic and International Studies. She is coauthor of *Local Content Requirements: A Global Problem* (2013).

Julia Muir was a research analyst at the Peterson Institute for International Economics from March 2010 to June 2013. She is currently a consultant at the Office of Integration and Trade, Inter-American Development Bank. Prior to joining the Institute she completed a Bachelor of Arts degree from McGill University with a concentration in international development studies and economics. She also holds a Master of Economics from the University of Sydney. She is coauthor of *Understanding the Trans-Pacific Partnership* (2012).

PETERSON INSTITUTE FOR INTERNATIONAL ECONOMICS
1750 Massachusetts Avenue, NW
Washington, DC 20036-1903
(202) 328-9000   FAX: (202) 659-3225
www.piie.com

Adam S. Posen, *President*
Steven R. Weisman, *Vice President for Publications and Communications*

Cover Design by Peggy Archambault
Cover Photo by © iStock Photo
Printing by Versa Press, Inc.

Printed in the United States of America
16   15   5   4   3   2

Library of Congress Cataloging-in-Publication Data
Hufbauer, Gary Clyde.
  Economic normalization with Cuba : a roadmap for US policymakers / Gary Clyde Hufbauer and Barbara Kotschwar.
    pages cm
  Includes bibliographical references.
  ISBN 978-0-88132-682-6
  1. United States—Foreign relations—Cuba.
2. Cuba—Foreign relations—United States. I. Kotschwar, Barbara. II. Title.
  E183.8.C9H84 2014
  327.7307291—dc23
                              2013050423

This publication has been subjected to a prepublication peer review intended to ensure analytical quality. The views expressed are those of the authors. This publication is part of the overall program of the Peterson Institute for International Economics, as endorsed by its Board of Directors, but it does not necessarily reflect the views of individual members of the Board or of the Institute's staff or management. The Institute is an independent, private, nonprofit institution for rigorous intellectually honest study and open discussion of international economic policy. Its work is made possible by financial support from a highly diverse group of philanthropic foundations, private corporations, and interested individuals, as well as by income on its capital fund. For a list of Institute supporters, please see www.piie.com/supporters.cfm.

Contents

Boxes

Preface

After more than a half century of distrust reinforced by tough economic sanctions imposed from Washington, Cuba and the United States may be ready for a new phase in their relationship. Unlikely as it might seem, *Economic Normalization with Cuba: A Roadmap for US Policymakers* by Gary Clyde Hufbauer and Barbara Kotschwar could not come at a better time.

The United States and Cuba have had extremely limited economic ties since the US commercial, economic, and financial embargo on Cuba was enacted in October 1960, a year after Fidel Castro and his revolutionaries overthrew the Batista military regime. In the period since then, Washington's main goal has been to destabilize if not overthrow the Castro regime, an effort that has not exactly been a ringing success. The Castro regime, meanwhile, has managed to survive as a Communist outpost in a region that has largely though not entirely turned to free markets.

Today, however, younger Cubans and Americans appear ready for more political and economic engagement. The regime of Raúl Castro, Fidel's brother, has allowed Cubans to buy and sell property, lifted restrictions on other private economic activity, and allowed more freedom of movement of individual Cubans within and outside the country. Raúl Castro has announced that he will retire in 2018. Recently, protests in Cuba have erupted, with Cubans demanding more liberalization. For its part, the United States, while continuing to criticize the Castro regime for its repression of basic civil and human rights, has quietly loosened restrictions on Cuban-American remittances to family members on the island and has opened the possibility of travel to Cuba to wider categories of Americans. Migration talks have resumed, and discussions on restarting direct mail service are ongoing.

Hufbauer and Kotschwar refrain from speculating on when or how political normalization will take place. Rather they lay out possible steps that US policymakers and businesses can take to restore normal—and reciprocal—economic relations with Cuba when the time comes and focus on the universe of economic and trade issues that will inform the terms and scope of normalization, once a high-level political decision had been made by the United States to move in that direction. While some argue that unconditional US withdrawal of sanctions offers the fastest path to Cuban economic progress, this book contends that reciprocal negotiations offers the best path toward both economic growth and deeper integration between the US and Cuban economies. First, drawing on the cautionary tales of other transition economies, the authors hold that reciprocal negotiations are necessary to tilt the political economy balance in favor of liberalization and mitigate the surge of vested interests that may resist modernization of the economy. Second, the authors hold that Cuba's embrace of all tenets of a market economy is the best path toward economic growth.

This study suggests constructive avenues for ensuring that the postembargo US-Cuba economic relationship starts on the right footing, with the door to commerce between the two countries opening in both directions. As dissident Cuban blogger Yoani Sanchez told an audience in Miami, "We are going to need each other for a future Cuba and we need each other in the present Cuba."[1] In this spirit, the authors set out a number of issues and sectors of economic importance and enumerate steps the US government should take to engage the Cuban government to liberalize trade, as well as reciprocal measures Cuba will need to take to ensure equal footing for US companies. The authors suggest several areas for liberalization, including medical tourism, agriculture, and energy. Importantly, the study offers a number of practical tools for advancing closer economic relations.

This study builds upon the Institute's long-standing work on economic sanctions, the keystone of which is the third edition of *Economic Sanctions Reconsidered* (Hufbauer, Jeffrey J. Schott, Kimberly Ann Elliot, and Barbara Oegg), with regular updates available on the website (www.piie.com). Cuba is an important case in this study of sanctions as an important yet highly controversial foreign policy tool.

The Peterson Institute for International Economics is a private, nonprofit institution for rigorous, intellectually open, and honest study and discussion of international economic policy. Its purpose is to identify and analyze important issues to making globalization beneficial and sustainable for the people of the United States and the world and then to develop and communicate practical new approaches for dealing with them. The Institute is completely nonpartisan.

---

1. Yoani Sanchez, "Cubans, period," text read at an event at the Freedom Tower, Miami, Florida, April 1, 2013, https://generacionyen.wordpress.com/2013/04/01/cubans-period.

The Institute's work is funded by a highly diverse group of philanthropic foundations, private corporations, and interested individuals, as well as income on its capital fund. About 35 percent of the Institute's resources in our latest fiscal year were provided by contributors from outside the United States. This study was made possible by the generous support of the Institute's general contributors, including the Bacardi Company, Caterpillar, Inc., and the Procter & Gamble Company.

The Executive Committee of the Institute's Board of Directors bears overall responsibility for the Institute's direction, gives general guidance and approval to its research program, and evaluates its performance in pursuit of its mission. The Institute's President is responsible for the identification of topics that are likely to become important over the medium term (one to three years) that should be addressed by Institute scholars. This rolling agenda is set in close consultation with the Institute's research staff, Board of Directors, and other stakeholders.

The President makes the final decision to publish any individual Institute study, following independent internal and external review of the work.

The Institute hopes that its research and other activities will contribute to building a stronger foundation for international economic policy around the world. We invite readers of these publications to let us know how they think we can best accomplish this objective.

ADAM S. POSEN
President
February 2014

Acknowledgments

The topic of Cuba is one that elicits much passion and on which there are sharply divided views. We were lucky to be able to count on cool and informed heads to help guide us through this process. This study benefited from the thoughtful insights and helpful guidance of a number of colleagues. We thank both Adam Posen and C. Fred Bergsten for encouraging us to carry it out. Dean DeRosa provided the basis for the analysis of trade and investment in chapter 6. We owe a particular debt to our colleagues Anders Åslund and Marc Noland, who took time from their busy schedules to share the wisdom of their knowledge and experience with transition economies and provide copious notes and well thought out comments on early drafts, which helped to significantly strengthen this study. We also wish to thank the participants of a study group session held in May 2013 and others who reviewed the work, particularly Richard Feinberg, Scott Miller, David Nelson, Ted Piccone, José Raúl Perales, Rafael Romeu, Chris Sabatini, Julia Sweig, and John Veroneau. All provided helpful guidance and comments as did two anonymous reviewers. We are especially grateful to Madona Devasahayam, Susann Luetjen, and Steve Weisman, who worked tirelessly to prepare this manuscript for publication.

This manuscript benefited from long conversations and excellent suggestions from Ed Tureen, PIIE's director of publications, who sadly passed away in May 2013. Ed treasured and drew upon his Cuban and American heritages as well as his keen eye for prose and knack for editing. We hope he would have been pleased with the results.

Map of Cuba and surrounding area

1

A Half Century of Separation

For more than 50 years the United States has opposed the Castro regime in Cuba, deploying both trade and financial sanctions. While this policy has not destabilized the Cuban government, the regime is showing signs of fatigue, and the sands of time may accomplish what economic sanctions did not. Fidel Castro, born in 1926, turned 87 on August 13, 2013, and actuarial tables give him a remaining life expectancy of 5 years.[1] Raúl Castro, born in 1931, now the president of Cuba, is 82 years old with a life expectancy of 7.5 years. Yet the Castro brothers are nothing if not durable, making the circumstances and timing of political normalization hard to forecast, but relations could be restored between the United States and Cuba within the space of years. In fact, on February 24, 2013, Raúl Castro announced he would step down as president, following a last five-year term ending in 2018.[2] Meanwhile, the regime

---

1. Fidel Castro's health has been deteriorating since 2006, when he underwent surgery for gastrointestinal bleeding. Since then, he has made only a handful of public appearances and in February 2008 stepped down from his role as president. In April 2011, he resigned from his role within the Communist Party, again for health reasons. Life expectancy figures quoted here are based on US mortality tables; Cuban male life expectancy at birth is about the same as in the United States, around 76 years.

2. Discurso pronunciado por el General de Ejército Raúl Castro Ruz, Primer Secretario del Comité Central del Partido Comunista de Cuba y Presidente de los Consejos de Estado y de Ministros, en la clausura de la Sesión Constitutiva de la Asamblea Nacional del Poder Popular, en su Octava Legislatura, y del Consejo de Estado, celebrada en el Palacio de Convenciones de La Habana, el 24 de febrero de 2013. [Speech by Commander in Chief of the Armed Forces Raúl Castro Ruz, first secretary of the Central Committee of the Communist Party of Cuba and president of the Council of State and of the Council of Ministers, in the closing session of the Constitutive Session of the National Assembly of People's Power in its eighth legislative session and of the Council of State in the Conventions Palace, Havana, February 24, 2013.]

is grooming Miguel Díaz-Canel, at 53 a relatively young first vice president, as a prospective new leader. Foretelling a new day, in his first term, President Barack Obama took small steps to relax the US embargo and permit more travel and remittances to Cuba.[3] In 2013, Cuba relaxed its exit permit system, permitting more Cubans to travel abroad.

Once *political normalization* is in sight, forces will emerge to urge instant *economic normalization*. But rushing to dismantle US sanctions and unilaterally opening US markets to Cuban goods and services, without proper institutions in place in Cuba and without dramatic liberalization of its own barriers to trade and investment, risks the loss of a golden moment to help US companies and their workers get a fair shake in the new Cuban economy. In our opinion, Cuba's full embrace of the tenets of a market economy and democratic institutions offers the best path forward for rapid Cuban economic growth. But this Policy Analysis is written foremost with an eye on US interests.

Much is at stake. The world has already witnessed Russia's headlong rush into capitalism, and the terrible consequences when an economy is captured by oligarchs and overrun by corruption, with only a veneer of democratic institutions.[4] For many Russians, the transition from communism to capitalism was a disaster. Without a proper institutional framework, much the same could happen in Cuba, given its huge portfolio of state-run companies closely tied to the military and its entrenched bureaucracy. US companies and workers have a legitimate interest in ensuring market access, respect for intellectual property, and investment opportunities in Cuba once Cuban firms are allowed to enjoy equivalent rights in the US market and access to US financial markets. Reciprocity of rights between Cuba and the United States is especially important since Cuba has already established trade and investment relations with Canadian, European, and, increasingly, Chinese firms. Without reciprocity, US companies and workers will continue to be disadvantaged, perhaps for several years.

This Policy Analysis is not about how the United States ought to rebuild Cuba or about the relative merits of the sanctions—two standard topics in this area—but rather a roadmap for how US businesses and policymakers could pursue US economic interests under the assumption that Cuba becomes a market economy—and perhaps adopts democratic institutions. We suggest markers for the path to restoring normal economic relations between the United States and Cuba, once a greater degree of political normalization is under way between the two countries.[5]

---

3. Cuba's show trial of Alan Gross, a US Agency for International Development subcontractor, in 2011 fueled opposition to the State Department's Cuba Democracy Program, and the conviction of Cuban spies also had a chilling effect, but on balance Cuba and the United States are inching toward political normalization. Chapters 2 and 3 provide details.

4. For a comprehensive discussion of the East European transitions, see Åslund (1992, 2013).

5. President Obama's modest steps in 2009 represented a degree of US economic liberalization in the absence of significant political reform in Cuba. We realize that overlaps will inevitably char-

This Policy Analysis focuses on the microeconomic grist of trade and investment relations between Cuba and the United States. To avoid utter chaos, Cuba will face severe macroeconomic challenges, whatever the transition scenario between an autocratic state-centered economy and a democratic market-centered economy. Cuba needs to establish a normal system of taxation and public expenditures and keep internal debt within reasonable bounds; it must unify its exchange rate, while managing the risk of hyperinflation; and it must settle its external debts, including claims arising from expropriated property, without landing in the impossible position Germany was in after the First World War. We touch only lightly on these challenges. The macroeconomic challenges are real, but overwhelmingly they will be the responsibility of Cuban officials.

The remainder of this chapter sets the context of Cuba's economy and outlines three stylized but plausible scenarios under which economic normalization could take place. Chapter 2 describes recent economic reforms in Cuba. Chapter 3 describes Cuba's extensive network of international economic agreements. Chapter 4 sketches the history and legislation of US economic sanctions against Cuba. Chapter 5 outlines potential initial steps toward the normalization of bilateral economic relations. Chapter 6 uses a gravity model and other tools to estimate potential trade and investment between Cuba and the United States. Chapter 7 describes additional agreements that would lead to deeper integration between the United States and Cuba. Chapter 8 concludes by recounting US "offensive" and "defensive" economic interests.

Cuban Fundamentals

For the past 50 years and counting, the Cuban economy has operated predominantly under a centrally planned system, controlled by the single-party communist government. Domestic production of goods is dominated by state-owned enterprises, while international trade and domestic consumption are tightly regulated by government institutions. The Cuban military, the Revolutionary Armed Forces, plays a major role in both the agricultural and service sectors. The Cuban economy has been shaped by the long-standing US commercial, economic, and financial embargo, initially imposed in 1960, strengthened in 1962, and reinforced by the Helms-Burton Act of 1996.

The dissolution in 1991 of the Council for Mutual Economic Assistance (CMEA), the Soviet trading bloc that Cuba joined in 1970, led to a sharp decline in Cuban output in the late 1980s and early 1990s. To arrest the sharp decline in GDP and personal income, the government took emergency economic measures, including liberalizing some activities, thus ushering in the "special period in peace time." However, many of the liberalization measures were rolled back, at least partially, in the early 2000s.

---

acterize political and economic normalization. In our view, however, significant political liberalization will need to precede the scope of economic normalization previewed in chapters 5 and 7.

Since 2000, Venezuela has stepped in to help Cuba with significant economic assistance. Through a so-called *Convenio Integral de Cooperación*, or comprehensive cooperation agreement, Venezuela provides Cuba with a significant amount of oil (between 90,000 and 130,000 barrels per day), at a 40 percent discount supplemented by a subsidized loan, the value of which is estimated at about $1.5 billion per year and covers about half of Cuba's energy needs (see, for example, Moody's Investor Service 2011). Cuba also receives payments for the export of medical personnel to serve in Venezuela's *misiones*; these payments are often estimated to be at a highly inflated value.[6] Venezuela has reportedly provided investment and development assistance as well, but the value of Venezuelan aid to Cuba is not transparently documented. Estimates range between $10 billion and $13 billion annually, or around 20 percent of Cuba's GDP during the past three years (Hernández-Catá 2013).[7]

In 2010 the government announced that it would be "updating" its economic model, encapsulated in the Draft Guidelines for Economic and Social Policy announced at the Sixth Cuban Communist Party Congress in October 2010. The new model contemplates incremental steps toward a market-oriented economy. These are detailed in chapter 2.

The Cuban economy is now largely a service economy. Services account for nearly three-quarters of the economy, while manufacturing accounts for 21 percent and agriculture just 5 percent (see table 1.1). Government services (e.g., education, health, and social services), coupled with nickel and cobalt mining and tourism, are the main contributors to GDP, which the Economist Intelligence Unit (EIU 2013) estimates at about $63 billion, or $71 billion at the official Cuban peso rate.[8] With a population of just over 11 million, the figures work out to a GDP of roughly $6,000 per capita. Because of massive distortions in the Cuban economy, including the highly distortive dual currency system, these GDP and per capita income figures must be taken with a tablespoon of salt.

6. Carmelo Mesa-Lago estimates the cost per doctor to be about $135,000 per year—far above salaries for doctors in Cuba (quoted in Nicholas Casey, "For Cuba, Chávez's Health Is a Vital Statistic," *Wall Street Journal*, June 22, 2012, http://online.wsj.com/article/SB10001424052702303879604577412190274916840.html).

7. The Cuba transition project of the University of Miami estimates Venezuela's assistance to Cuba at about $10 billion per year (Lopez 2012). Mesa-Lago (2009) has estimated the value of the 2008 subsidies at about $9.4 billion.

8. Around 1990, Cuba began to measure its GDP using the System of National Accounts (SNA) methodology, rather than the Material Product System (MPS). Since 2003, Cuba has included the value of government services, a major component of the Cuban economy, by using an estimate of the market value of the services, rather than valuing them at cost, the measure used in the standard SNA method. Serious questions have been raised about the reliability of official Cuban GDP statistics. For one, the Cuban government continues to use 1981 as a base year for the accounts; for another, the Cuban economy suffers from severe price distortions resulting from significant use of subsidies and a wildly distorted dual exchange rate system. See, for example, Pérez-López and Mesa-Lago (2009).

Table 1.1 Cuban economic indicators, 2012

Indicator	Value
GDP (current billions of US dollars)	71.0
GDP per capita (current US dollars)	6,288
Composition of GDP (percent)[a]	
Agriculture	5
Industry	21
Services	74
Population (millions)	11.3
Gross enrollment (percent)[b]	80
Tertiary education	80
Secondary education	90
Unemployment (percent)	3.8
Exports (billions of US dollars)	
Goods	6.0
Services	10.2
Imports (billions of US dollars)	
Goods	13.7
Services	2.3
Inward FDI stock, estimate (millions of US dollars)	427

FDI = foreign direct investment

a. Composition of GDP data from 2010.
b. Gross enrollment is the total enrollment, regardless of age, expressed as a percentage of the population of official school age. Data from 2011.

Sources: GDP, GDP per capita, and unemployment figures from Economic Commission of Latin America and the Caribbean (ECLAC), www.eclac.org/deype/default.asp?idioma=IN; composition of GDP, population, and education figures from World Bank, *World Development Indicators* database, http://data.worldbank.org/indicator; export and import data from World Trade Organization Statistics Database, Cuba Trade Profile, http://stat.wto.org/CountryProfile/WSDBCountryPFView.aspx?Language=E&Country=CU; FDI data from UNCTAD (2012).

Cuba ranks well on social indicators. Cubans are relatively well educated: Cuba has the highest literacy levels in Latin America. Some 90 percent of school-aged children are enrolled in secondary education, and 80 percent of the relevant cohort is enrolled in tertiary education. Cuba reports very low levels of unemployment, just 3.8 percent in 2012. However, this statistic reflects the fact that 78 percent of the labor force is employed by the government at very low wages.[9] It also ignores the skills mismatch in the labor force: It is not

---

9. This is beginning to change: In 2010 Raúl Castro announced his intention to let go about half a million government employees by mid-2011 and reduce restrictions on private enterprise to help the erstwhile government employees find new jobs. To date, private employment has been allowed

unusual to find Cuban taxi drivers or waiters with advanced degrees in medicine or engineering. Cuba also faces a demographic challenge with an aging population. The over-65 population accounts for 13 percent of the total, while the under-14 population accounts for only 17 percent. This contrasts with the rest of Latin America, which is poised to collect a demographic dividend, since only 7 percent of the population is above 65, while 28 percent is 14 or younger.

A long life expectancy for Cubans (80 years for women, 76 for men), together with low birth rates and the outward migration of a significant portion of its working population (many to the United States, which issues a minimum of 20,000 visas per year to Cubans [Wasem 2012]), imposes a heavy burden on the economically active population. This raises concerns for a state that has long been proud of providing free and universal access to health care and education along with other benefits. The economic difficulties of the 1990s eroded Cuba's significant achievement in these social indicators: During the "special period," the education budget was slashed by nearly 40 percent. Poor transportation infrastructure made attendance more difficult, resulting in falling participation rates for secondary and tertiary students. Difficulties in finding employment and low state sector wages also contributed to declines in university attendance. Fewer resources in the health sector have also led to poorer service, although a parallel health sector for tourists with hard currency has maintained a higher quality standard (Mesa-Lago 2011, 52).

Cuba has a merchandise trade deficit—7.6 billion CUCs (Cuba's convertible peso, set at par to the dollar) in 2011, according to Cuba's National Office of Statistics. The economy relies heavily on imports of essential goods such as petroleum, food, machinery and equipment, and chemicals. Exports have remained relatively flat over the past five years, largely due to lagging productivity, only picking up in 2011 to reach about $6 billion in 2012. Cuban merchandise exports are mainly commodities: sugar, tobacco, coffee, nickel, some fish, and citrus fruits. Cuba, however, is a large exporter of services, officially reported as $10 billion in 2010, making services an important source of foreign exchange.[10] The majority of these exports are tourist and medical services, many exchanged through barter arrangements in initiatives with Venezuela such as the Bolivarian Alliance for the Peoples of Our America (ALBA) trade agreement. Barter trade has taken on an increasing role in the Cuban economy: Luis R. Luis (2012) estimates that barter trade has expanded from about 40 percent of overall merchandise trade in 2008 to about 60 percent in 2010. A reported 40,000 Cuban doctors work in 66 countries in Africa, Asia, and Latin America (the majority of them are in Venezuela, as discussed

---

in about 180 economic activities and the private sector has expanded from about 180,000 to about 400,000 people.

10. The prices attributed to Cuban exports of medical sources are very likely exaggerated to conceal (from the Venezuelan public) the implicit subsidy in petroleum deliveries and other assistance to Cuba. An estimated 30,000 Cuban doctors and other medical personnel work in Venezuela in exchange for an estimated 90,000 to 130,000 barrels a day of oil sold at preferential rates.

above). The EIU (2008, 42) places the value of nontourism services, largely comprising professional services, at about $3 billion. Cuba's trade minister, Rodrigo Malmierca, recently cited Cuban doctors working abroad as a main source of foreign exchange and a key future growth industry.[11] Whether Cuba can export Cuban professional services—especially doctors—to countries other than Venezuela on a large scale remains to be seen. Brazil recently signed a deal to bring in 4,000 Cuban doctors by the end of 2013 to improve faltering public health services and address the short supply of medical personnel.[12] These doctors will be posted to remote or poor areas, which generally suffer from inadequate facilities and equipment and crumbling infrastructure. But many fault the Brazilian government for an underfunded and low-quality healthcare system and question whether the import of Cuban doctors can serve as a long-term solution. The arrival of these Cuban doctors caused some friction between the government and the medical community.

A compelling question is whether Venezuela will continue to honor its concessions to Cuba. Two weeks after taking office, Venezuela's President Nicolas Maduro reaffirmed his commitment to the strategic alliance with Cuba and signed 51 cooperation agreements with an estimated value of $1 billion. However, if the world price of oil declines substantially, an overall commitment totaling $10 billion annually seems unlikely, especially now that President Hugo Chávez has passed into history and Venezuela is experiencing severe economic troubles at home. China has also helped sustain the Cuban regime with interest-free loans, credit lines, and investment in Cuba's petroleum infrastructure. China has also invested in health infrastructure, helped upgrade hospitals and research facilities, and helped build Venezuela's ALBA broadband cable, a fiber optic cable stretching from Venezuela to Cuba—part of Venezuela's "goodwill" aid to Cuba.

Foreign direct investment (FDI) in Cuba has ebbed and flowed ever since the Soviet Union withdrew its financial support in the early 1990s. To make up for the annual subsidies formerly received from the Soviet Union,[13] Cuba implemented minor market-oriented reforms in the 1990s to spur inward FDI. These included developing the tourism industry, with new hotels built along the beachfronts, often by Spanish companies. Licenses for self-employment were issued on a limited basis, largely to small entities supplying tourism services. Oil, gas, mining, biotech, and pharmaceuticals were at least partially opened up to foreign investment, and the main sectors for inward FDI have

---

11. Carlos Batista, "Doctors reap in billions as Cuba's top export," Agence France-Presse, June 19, 2013, http://uk.news.yahoo.com/doctors-reap-billions-cubas-top-export-165058312.html#5yz-TInT (accessed on October 11, 2013).

12. Paula Moura and Juan Forero, "Brazil, facing health-care crisis, imports Cuban doctors," *Washington Post*, August 30, 2013, http://articles.washingtonpost.com/2013-08-30/world/ 41602462 _1_cuban-doctors-health-system-brazilian-doctors (accessed on September 16, 2013).

13. Soviet subsidies were estimated at about 20 to 30 percent of GDP. See Hernández-Catá (2012) and Ritter (1990).

been nickel mining, oil, tourism, and telecommunications. However, during the early 2000s, once the Cuban economy experienced a small recovery (assisted in large part by Venezuelan aid), the government went through a phase of retrenchment and ordered the closure of numerous joint ventures.

Cuba's current economic environment is not particularly conducive to foreign investors and, in 2011, the reported FDI stock was only $427 million (UNCTAD 2012) with flows totaling about $30 to $35 million per year (ECLAC 2011). The main investors are still Europe and Canada but Brazil and China have become major investors, both of which offer lines of credit for their firms to gain a foothold (see, for example, Luis 2009).[14] The government is slow to approve new joint ventures or authorize investors to move forward on existing projects. One concern is that foreign-invested projects might compete with state enterprises; another concern is that market forces might undermine the prevailing socialist ideology. However, if the scope of Venezuelan assistance shrinks, Cuba might renew its charm offensive with foreign investors.

A major structural challenge facing Cuba is the elimination of its dual currency system, which has been in place since 1993 and is now slated to be phased out.[15] Following the collapse of the Soviet Union, Cuba legalized the possession and use of US dollars. US dollars flowed freely in Cuba until 2004, when, in response to US administrative tightening of its embargo, the government banned their use in shops and other businesses.[16] US dollars were replaced by the convertible peso, or CUC, sometimes referred to on the street as the "dollar" or *chavito*, which is pegged to the US dollar at $1.00 per peso.[17] A fee of 10 percent is applied on conversion of CUCs into dollars.

Cuba's other official currency is the national peso, or CUP. State workers receive most of their wages in national pesos, with a small portion paid in convertible pesos. Basic stores, accessible to the entire population, accept the national peso, while "dollar shops" accept only convertible pesos. While the official exchange rate between the CUC and the CUP is one-to-one, only the CUC is convertible and actually trades at about 25 CUPs.[18]

---

14. In 2010, for example, China and Cuba announced 13 joint projects, 7 in the Cuban mechanical industry, communications, agriculture, tourism, biotechnology, and health sectors (ECLAC 2011).

15. An official note published in *Granma Internacional* on October 22, 2013, states that Cuba will "advance toward monetary unification, taking into account the productivity of labor and effectiveness of distributive and redistributive mechanisms. Given its complexity, this process demands rigorous preparation and execution, on both the subjective and objective planes." See www.granma.cu/ingles/news-i/22oct-43notaoficial.html.

16. In May 2004, the US Federal Reserve fined Swiss bank UBS $100 million for violating US trade sanctions by sending US dollars to Cuba.

17. From April 2008 to March 2011 the peso was revalued to $1.08 per peso.

18. The Cadeca rate, established by the state foreign exchange agency, which governs household sector transactions, is set at 25 CUPs equals 1 CUC. This rate is applied to personal transactions.

This dual exchange rate system confers a substantial subsidy on the state, which pays most salaries in CUPs, at one-25th the value of CUCs. It also makes a realistic understanding of Cuba's economic situation very difficult. The CUP is the currency that most Cubans use for daily transactions. At the official rate of one-to-one, per capita GDP is just over $6,000 (the figure generally reported), which places Cuba in the World Bank's upper-middle-income category. However, if CUPs were translated at the unofficial exchange rate of 25 CUPs equals 1 CUC, per capita GDP would fall to $240, which would place Cuba with countries such as Burundi and Ethiopia. The truth is between these two extremes but probably well below $6,000 per capita.

The dual exchange rate system is blamed for fostering inequality among Cubans. About 40 percent of the population has little or no access to the convertible peso, and the average Cuban monthly wage is about 440 national pesos, or about 18 CUCs. Cubans with access to CUCs, such as those who work in the tourism sector or those who receive remittances, are a privileged class, enjoying access to a much wider range of goods and services. ECLAC estimates remittances at about $1 billion per year. Surveys such as those conducted by Manuel Orozco (2009) place remittances between $800 million and $1,200 million. However, some analysts estimate 2011 remittances at more than $2 billion per year (Morales and Scarpaci 2012).

On October 22, 2013, Cuba's state media announced that the Council of Ministers had approved a timetable (not yet made public) for implementing monetary unification The Cuban government has recognized the deleterious effect of the dual currency system on the economy, acknowledging that:

> As has been stated, monetary and currency exchange unification is not a measure which will, in itself, resolve all of the economy's current problems, but its implementation is indispensable to reestablishing the value of the Cuban peso and its function as money; that is to say, as a unit of accounting, payment and savings. This measure, in conjunction with other policies directed toward the updating of our model, will allow for the ordering of the economic environment and, consequently, the accurate measurement of its performance.[19]

Even before embarking on monetary unification, Cuba has already taken small steps to better align the domestic economy with global prices.[20] In 2010, as part of the "update" of its economic model, the government allowed hundreds of establishments to sell goods and provide services in national pesos. This was seen as a small measure toward phasing out the dual currency system.

---

19. Official note in *Granma Internacional*, October 22, 2013, www.granma.cu/ingles/news-i/22oct-43notaoficial.html.

20. These were acknowledged by President Raúl Castro late in 2012: "Valoramos que la actualización del modelo económico marcha con paso seguro y se empieza a adentrar en cuestiones de mayor alcance" ["We value that the updated economic model is proceeding steadily and is beginning to delve into broader issues"], *Granma Internacional*, December 14, 2012, www.granma.cubaweb.cu/2012/12/14/nacional/artic09.html.

In early 2013, Cuba adopted a pilot project in which some firms can use exchange rates ranging from CUP11:CUC1 to CUP7:CUC1 (EIU 2013). The government has not yet published concrete proposals for the unification but has put forth a number of principles. The process will first affect incorporated entities, building upon the pilot project. This will lead to the development of a legal framework and changes in accounting practices coupled with training of those charged with implementing the changes. The official note also pledges that "no monetary measure will be adopted to the detriment of those who lawfully obtain their income in CUCs or CUPs. In this instance, the process of monetary unification will respect the principle that the confidence shown by persons who have kept their savings in Cuban banks in CUCs, other international currencies, or CUPs, will remain intact." For the moment, the exchange rate of 25 CUPs to 1 CUC will remain in force. Given the enormous value gap between the CUC and the CUP, going to parity quickly at anywhere near the official one-to-one rate would sharply increase the demand for CUC-priced goods and possibly lead to hyperinflation with widespread food shortages. For example, according to economist Carmelo Mesa-Lago, just an 8:1 conversion ratio between the CUP and the CUC would triple government expenditures on salaries, a sure route to high inflation.[21]

Very likely, any convergence of CUP into CUCs at a rate more favorable than 25:1 would result in a significant devaluation of the CUC, severely impacting corporate balance sheets, which are expressed in dollars and assume parity between the CUP, the CUC, and the dollar. The blow would be felt by state-owned enterprises, joint venture companies, and government entities, all of which use the CUC. The implications of alternative exchange rate systems are beyond the scope of this Policy Analysis.[22] Suffice it to say that a severe macroeconomic shock will probably accompany exchange rate unification if CUPs are converted into CUCs at a rate anywhere near one-to-one.

Another constraint on the economy is external debt. Cuba defaulted on its external debt in 1960 and has done so several times subsequently, including in 1986. Since the early 1980s, Cuba has taken steps to renegotiate portions of its debt and is generally seen as honoring the terms of the new debt restructuring agreements (Pérez 2008).[23] The Central Bank of Cuba reports a total debt of

---

21. Tom Cleveland, "Analysis: The dual-currency system will take years to resolve," *Cuba Standard*, June 25, 2012, www.cubastandard.com/2012/06/25/analysis-the-dual-currency-system-will-take-years-to-resolve (accessed on October 11, 2013).

22. See, for example, Pérez (2008) and Di Bella and Wolfe (2008) for more on this issue.

23. In recent years, Cuba has taken steps to honor part of its prior debt obligations. For example, in 2012 Cuba settled a dispute with Japanese commercial creditors in which 80 percent of the 130 billion yen debt ($1.4 billion) was forgiven while the remainder will be paid over 20 years. Germany also broke with the Paris Club and signed a bilateral agreement covering $115 million in debt, with short-term loans to be paid through 2003 and medium- and long-term to be paid between 2006 and 2020. This agreement enabled Germany to resume offering Hermes export credit guarantees. In May 2012, Germany raised the ceiling for its export credits, based on Cuba's repayment record,

$17.82 billion, which is likely understated: Outside estimates range between $23 billion (EIU 2013) and $35 billion (Paris Club 2013). The amounts officially stated by Cuba exclude debt to Russia, China, Vietnam, and the Czech Republic.[24] One challenge in estimating the value of Cuba's foreign debt is determining the "right" exchange rate for converting into dollars Cuba's debt to the former Soviet Union, since inherited by Russia. Excluding Russian debt, Cuba's foreign debt has been estimated between 30 and 40 percent of GDP (Pérez 2008).

Settlement of Claims

In this Policy Analysis we do not address in depth the politics of US sanctions or the settlement of claims, both charged and intertwined topics that have been covered elsewhere.[25] Nevertheless we recognize that claims will be a central question in the normalization of political relations. US corporate compensation claims, and Cuban-American compensation claims, for property that was seized, initially in 1959 and 1960 and later as Cubans fled the island, are substantial. The Joint Corporate Committee on Cuban Claims, a nonprofit organization comprising entities whose claims have been certified by the US Foreign Claims Settlement Commission, estimates that the value of corporate claims was approximately $1.8 billion at the time they were seized.[26] Taking inflation into account since the commission rendered its verdict in 1972, more than 40 years ago, the current value of these claims could be as high as $10 billion.

Moreover, to the claims of corporations must be added the claims of Cuban-Americans—persons who held Cuban citizenship when they fled the island and had their property seized in the 1960s, 1970s, and 1980s. The total magnitude is unknown, but since 1.1 million persons of Cuban birth are now American citizens, and since most of them lost everything when they left Cuba,

---

from 20 million to 25 million euros for short-term (up to one year) export credits and from 40 million to 45 million euros for medium- and long-term credits. In early 2013 it was reported that Cuba and Russia had come to an agreement on some measure of debt forgiveness that would be finalized in 2014 ("Russia to write off $35 billion of Cuba's debt," Pravda.ru, February 22, 2013, http://english.pravda.ru/russia/economics/22-02-2013/123875-russia_cuba_debt-0/ [accessed on July 14, 2013]; "Russia-Cuba debt deal creates waves among creditors," Reuters, March 14, 2013, www.reuters.com/article/2013/03/14/cuba-debt-russia-idUSL1N0C592Z20130314 [accessed on July 14, 2013]). Details have not been made public as of this writing.

24. Small debts to South Africa ($13 million) for diesel engines and to Chile ($20 million) for mackerel imports are also excluded ("Slippery, shapeless and slow to be repaid," *Economist*, May 17, 2001, www.economist.com/node/624002 [accessed on May 31, 2013]).

25. See Carter (2008), Drury (2000), Selden (1999), Gavin (1989), and Kaempfer and Lowenberg (1988).

26. Some 8,816 claims were presented to the Foreign Claims Settlement Commission between 1966 and 1972. The commission certified 5,911 claims as valid. More than 85 percent of the total value of claims ($1.58 billion) corresponded to 898 corporate claims.

the sum must be very large (see Motel and Patten 2012).[27] On the other hand, once Cuba fully normalizes its economic relations with the United States and other trading partners, the Cuban economy should grow rapidly, making the settlement of claims an easier task for the Cuban government. Rapid growth was the common experience of socialist economies in Asia (China and Vietnam) and Europe (Poland, Czechoslovakia, and others) once they adopted market policies.

Matías F. Travieso-Díaz (1997, 2002), José A. Ortiz (2000), and Rolando Anillo-Badia (2011), among others, examine the legal basis for expropriation claims of US nationals and possible avenues for resolution. The established principles of international law recognize "the sovereign right of states to expropriate the assets of foreign nationals" but also require "prompt, adequate and effective compensation to aliens whose property is expropriated" (Travieso-Díaz 2002). Moreover, the Cuban law that authorized the expropriation of property of US nationals contained provisions that required the government to provide adequate compensation to property owners. While Cuba has settled claims by other foreign nationals, such as those in Spain and Switzerland, it has not resolved claims by US nationals. However, these earlier settlements did not adhere to the "prompt, adequate and effective" compensation principles established in international law. Instead, lump sum payments were negotiated over long periods of time and were far short of amounts claimed by individual nationals (Travieso-Díaz 2002).

Historically the United States has settled expropriation claims through government-to-government negotiations, and settlements have required payments to the US government, which are then distributed to claimants in proportion to their claim. The payments typically reflect only the principal amount of claims (no interest) and are typically a fraction of the estimated value of confiscated assets, well under 40 percent (Anillo-Badia 2011). Individual claimants may not opt out of the settlement reached by the US government and may not pursue claims either in US courts or in the settling country.

A lump sum cash payment—even at a fraction of total claims—may not be a viable option for Cuba given the large amounts outstanding. Alternative options include payment over a reasonable period of time (say, 10 years), direct restitution of property seized, or alternative forms of compensation such as the exchange of claims for investment opportunities in state-owned enterprises or real estate.[28]

In our view, at the next stage of political normalization, the US and Cuban government should establish a new claims commission, operating under established US precedents, to evaluate the claims of Cuban-Americans whose properties were seized by Cuba over the past 50 years. In nearly all cases, the

---

27. If the average claim for each Cuban-born American was just $5,000, the total would exceed $5 billion.

28. For a detailed exposition of alternatives, see Travieso-Díaz (1997, 2002), Ortiz (2000), and Anillo-Badia (2011).

remedy should be dollar compensation rather than direct restitution of residential property. Smaller claims (say, under $10,000) should be settled in cash, while larger claims should be paid over time or in certificates exchangeable for interests in Cuban state-owned property.

Leaving aside the important issue of claims, over the next few years, several possible paths can be envisaged for political and economic reforms within Cuba. To keep our discussion within bounds, we offer stylized outlines of three possible scenarios: gradualist normalization with continuing single-party dominance; big bang political change accompanied by monopolistic capitalism and grudging reforms; and big bang normalization accompanied by all the tenets of a market economy. Historical examples exist for all three scenarios. Whatever the scenario, Cuba will face the macroeconomic challenges mentioned earlier—taxation, public expenditure, and internal debt; unification of the exchange rate; and settlement of external claims.

Gradualist Normalization

The path overwhelmingly preferred by Cuban leaders starting with Raúl Castro is captured by the term "gradualism." The foremost model for this scenario is China over the past two decades, but Vietnam is a current practitioner of gradualism. Along this path, economic reforms will occur step by step, with close study of each step. Critically, a single party will continue to control Cuban politics but allow slow liberalization. Inevitably the gradualism path will entail more overlap between political and economic normalization than either of the "big bang" scenarios.

Following a path of gradualist normalization, the first steps, which have already been taken by the Raúl Castro administration, are legal permission for Cubans to buy and sell homes and cars and to open small shops. State-owned enterprises (SOEs) are already allowed to form joint ventures with foreign firms. If gradualism continues to be the way forward, the challenge for the United States will be to link each step forward in the normalization of US economic ties with appropriate measures to ensure that US firms and workers gain additional rights in the Cuban economy. Three concrete examples illustrate this path:

- If the United States freely permits Americans to travel to Cuba as pleasure tourists—a step that could bring billions of dollars annually to the Cuban economy—then Cuba should ensure that US hotel and resort chains can operate on an equal footing with Cuban and European establishments. The same principle applies to American medical tourists and Cuban health clinics.

- If the United States consents to Cuban membership in the International Monetary Fund (IMF), and hence the World Bank, then Cuba should set a timetable for remedying any shortfall in its obligations under the World Trade Organization (WTO) and other international organizations, such as the World Intellectual Property Organization (WIPO).

- If Cuban firms are allowed (by their own government and the US government) to sell goods and services in the United States—for example, cigars, spirits, fruits, or software—then US firms should be allowed to sell the same range of goods and services in Cuba. Likewise, if Cuban firms are allowed to invest in the United States, then to the same extent US firms should be allowed to invest in Cuba.[29] Under the current Cuban rulebook, joint ventures must be authorized by the Cuban government. US companies should receive treatment equally favorable to those of countries already operating in Cuba in any FDI decision making process. FDI has traditionally been limited to a narrow range of sectors while others—for example, sugar—have been off limits. Cuban officials should refrain from setting restrictions on the areas of main interest to US companies.

Big Bang with Monopoly Capitalism

Another scenario, illustrated by Russia and the Ukraine, is big bang political change, in which capitalism quickly replaces state ownership, but monopolies and oligopolies soon control the "commanding heights" of the economy and the new owners fiercely resist reforms that would foster competition. A big bang of this sort may have a veneer of democratic institutions, but it will tend toward autocratic leadership. In this scenario, the United States will need to scramble to help Cuba establish basic institutions and the rule of law in the brief period before autocratic leaders and monopoly capitalists establish a firm grip. During that brief period, Cuba might enact serious market-oriented reforms. Once the period passes, vested interests within Cuba will make it very difficult to get the rules and institutions right. In this scenario, the challenge not only for the United States but also for countries that have already established their investments in Cuba, such as Brazil, Canada, and Spain, is to ensure that behind-the-border barriers and anticompetitive practices do not flourish. Instead, world standards for commercial and intellectual property should become part of Cuban law, all foreign firms should enjoy most favored nation (MFN) access to investment opportunities and services markets, and the rule of law should become the norm, for both the civil and criminal courts.

It will be especially important that Cuban regulators not be "captured" by their respective industries. For example, banking regulation should not create exclusive niches for certain firms in mortgage lending and credit cards, port and airport regulators should keep physical infrastructure open to aircraft and ships of all flags, competition should be welcomed in the provision of mobile phones, and so on, sector by sector.

---

29. Since US investments in Cuba can be stalled or blocked by a slow-moving Cuban bureaucracy and an array of permits, equivalent treatment for US firms will require close monitoring of implementation, not just formal legal declarations of open access. Cuban investments in the United States are, of course, currently blocked by sanctions, but when these are relaxed there do not appear to be investment restraints from the Cuban side.

Big Bang with Market Capitalism

A third stylized scenario, the one most aligned with US interests, is big bang political reform coupled with Cuba's embrace of the core tenets of a market economy. This is the path that Poland and the three Baltic states followed when Soviet control ended in 1990. The Raúl Castro government and officials who control SOEs dread this scenario the most. Their antipathy commends the stylized scenario, but our reading of Cuban tea leaves reveals it is the least likely of the three. We could be wrong.

If big bang political reform is coupled with Cuba's own embrace of market capitalism, the need for the United States to pursue a reciprocal approach to normalization will almost disappear. Of its own accord Cuba will enact nearly all the reforms outlined in chapters 5 and 7 of this Policy Analysis and the United States can gladly implement the "concessions" detailed in those chapters. The main thing left to negotiate will be a comprehensive bilateral free trade agreement, to deal with a few outstanding issues and to guard against backsliding.

If our reading of Cuban tea leaves suggested that this scenario was most likely, this Policy Analysis would have been much shorter. We could have simply copied from the Polish playbook and listed everything that Cuba and the United States would automatically change to establish the sort of cordial commercial relationship that now exists between the United States and Poland or between the United States and Mexico. The Policy Analysis could have concluded by pointing out a few loose ends that remain to be tidied up. But because our reading suggests that either gradualism or monopoly capitalism is a more likely scenario, we have authored a detailed step-by-step roadmap.

We recommend constructive avenues for ensuring that the postembargo US-Cuba economic relationship starts on the right footing. We suggest how trade and investment relations between the United States and Cuba should be conducted—assessing the use of instruments such as loans and grants by the World Bank and the Inter-American Development Bank, free trade agreements and bilateral investment treaties, and implementation of Cuba's obligations as a member of the WTO and other international organizations. We explore the interaction of these international pacts with Cuban institutional reform and Cuban economic activities such as tourism, energy, sugar, spirits, health care, and air rights.

2

Cuban Economic Reforms

Before drilling down to instruments and activities for normalizing future commercial relations between the United States and Cuba, it is useful to place the postembargo Cuba-US economic relationship in its historical context, by examining Cuba's past and recent measures toward economic reform.

Cuba has seen two major periods of economic reform aimed at increasing productivity, decreasing its reliance on imports, improving access to foreign credit, and reducing the role of government in the economy. The first was in the early 1990s, when the collapse of the Soviet Union cut off a main source of funds and unhinged the carefully constructed system of bilateral economic agreements and barter arrangements through which Cuba had inserted itself into the international economy. The second is Cuba's current policy of *actualización*, or updating its economy to bring Cuban economic fundamentals more in line with the realities of the global economic environment. This phase began after 2006, when Raúl Castro assumed the role of president. Castro acknowledged some inefficiencies in Cuba's economy and recognized the need for "structural and conceptual changes."[1]

Special Period, 1990–2000

Cuba's reliance on subsidies from the Soviet Union left it extremely vulnerable to the changes that swept through the Soviet bloc in the late 1980s and early 1990s (Erikson 2009, 233–35). Fidel Castro foreshadowed the tough economic times that would follow the fall of the Berlin Wall in 1989, declaring that Cuba

---

1. Raúl Castro, "Year 49 of the Revolution," speech at Camagüey, Cuba, July 26, 2007, www.cadenagramonte.cu (accessed on May 1, 2013).

was entering a "special period in a time of peace."[2] Cuban trade collapsed and GDP declined by about a third between 1991 and 1994. The special period was marked by scarcity of foreign exchange, electricity, water, medicines, and food. Cars were replaced by Chinese bicycles. Economic hardship was compounded by a tightening of the US embargo in 1992, which led to scores of Cubans escaping the island on homemade rafts, the so-called *balsero* crisis.[3]

In response to the special period, the Cuban government began to ease restrictions on economic activity of its citizens. To stimulate production and consumption, the government implemented reforms related to (1) employment, (2) agricultural production and private enterprise, and (3) foreign capital and investment.

In terms of labor policy, the government legalized self-employment in over 100 occupations (Laverty 2009). This gave rise to a spate of barbershops, auto mechanics, small bed and breakfast establishments, and small private restaurants known as *paladares*. These were restricted to self-employment and hiring limited numbers of family members; adding nonfamily employees was not allowed. The relaxation of labor and employment laws helped absorb some of the workers displaced when the economy contracted in the post-Soviet years. By 1996, some 200,000 individuals had obtained licenses for self-employment (Laverty 2009).

In the agricultural sector, the government allowed public land to be converted to semiprivate cooperatives. The government also allowed farmers to sell any excess produce in private farmers' markets at unregulated prices. Some of these cooperatives and farmers' markets have managed to survive the subsequent retrenchment and they form the foundation for further agricultural reforms.

The government enacted new measures to facilitate inward foreign direct investment (FDI). In 1992 the Cuban Constitution was amended to allow property ownership and the transfer of state property to joint ventures with foreign investors. Investors from Canada, Mexico, Spain, and other European countries responded by entering the Cuban market, mostly in the tourism and natural resource sectors. The government also enacted amendments to improve the ease of doing business. For example, joint ventures were exempted from taxes on gross income, personal income, and the transfer of real estate and business property. The government also removed restrictions on hiring foreign executives, eliminated customs duties for certain essential goods and equipment, and allowed 51 percent foreign ownership in special cases. Although Fidel Castro

---

2. The Cuban government was not as prescient about the politics of the period, opposing the changes enacted by Mikhail Gorbachev and maintaining steadfast commitment to the preservation of socialism (see Erikson 2009, 233–35; Domínguez et al. 2012, 34–35).

3. In the summer of 1994 a riot off Havana harbor prompted the Cuban government to allow emigration by boat or raft to the United States. This led to the negotiations of a new set of immigration agreements between Cuba and the United States that remain in force at this writing.

had long been opposed to tourism, restrictions on inbound travel were lifted and thousands of visitors from Canada and Europe started to pour in.

In 1995, the government took further steps to attract FDI, through the enactment of the Foreign Investment Act (Law 77 of 1995 on Foreign Investment). The Act theoretically permitted FDI in all sectors of the Cuban economy except defense, education, and health care. It expanded the type of FDI permitted, allowing (1) joint ventures, (2) international economic association contracts (EACs), and (3) 100 percent foreign ownership (full foreign ownership company). The Act also created duty-free zones and industrial parks open to foreign investors. Most importantly the Act made expropriation illegal, except for specific cases of "public interest," in which case compensation to foreign investors was required. Foreign investments in Cuba, once preliminary agreements are concluded with the Cuban counterpart or the relevant Cuban ministry or ministries, are subject to a five-step approval process that entails (1) the conclusion of a feasibility study and negotiation of main corporate documents; (2) submission of a proposal to the ministry in charge of the sector in which the investment will take place; (3) presentation of the proposal to the Ministry of Foreign Investment and Economic Collaboration as well as to the ministry overseeing the sector in which the investment will take place; (4) consultation with all relevant government bodies; and (5) presentation of the final proposal to the Executive Committee of the Council of Ministers for their final approval. The Foreign Investment Act stipulates that approval or denial should be granted within 60 days of acceptance by the Ministry of Foreign Investment and Economic Collaboration as set out in step 3.[4]

Another important market reform was legalization of the US dollar in 1993.[5] This allowed Cubans to possess and spend US dollars in stores previously restricted to foreigners, giving Cubans access to a greater variety of services and goods that were not rationed in the same manner as those traded through the peso. Legalization of the dollar also allowed Cubans to receive remittances from relatives living abroad and helped relieve some of the shortages resulting from scarce foreign currency. By the mid-1990s, remittances from Cuban-Americans ranked with sugar and tourism as the top earners of foreign exchange (Domínguez et al. 2012, 36). While the use of the US dollar created opportunities, this multiple exchange rate system also introduced severe market distortions, which increased inequality between, on the one hand, Cubans who enjoyed access to US dollars—principally those working in the newly generated tourism jobs who received tips from foreigners, together with Cubans who received remittances from abroad—and, on the other hand, Cubans who had no access to US dollars.

---

4. The English translation of Law 77 is available at CubaIndustria, www.cubaindustria.cu/English/law_77.htm.

5. Douglas Farah, "Cuba Opts to Legalize the Dollar," *Washington Post*, July 25, 1993, A01, www.washingtonpost.com (accessed on May 6, 2013).

Backsliding, Late 1990s to Early 2000s

The positive effects of market reforms were short-lived. During the late 1990s and early 2000s, the government began to backtrack on reforms implemented earlier. For example, the government began to limit self-employment licensing and eventually stopped issuing licenses altogether (Laverty 2009, Peters 2006). The government also implemented a series of taxes and regulations that stifled private microenterprises, which had previously flourished through the system of self-employment. In 2004, the government withdrew the US dollar from circulation and introduced the convertible Cuban peso (CUC). Dollars could no longer be used to purchase goods and services. Instead, all dollar transactions had to be conducted using the CUC, meaning Cubans had to convert their US dollars into CUCs at a one-to-one rate but after paying a 10 percent surcharge (essentially a tax on dollars).[6] Cubans were still permitted to hold US dollars and dollar-denominated bank accounts but could not make new deposits into those accounts. These new provisions somewhat reduced the inflow of remittances.

Raúl Castro Reforms, 2006 to Present

The next wave of economic reforms began in the mid-2000s, when Raúl Castro temporarily took over as acting president in 2006 and then was elected president in 2008, when Fidel Castro permanently withdrew from office. Raúl publicly acknowledged deficiencies in the Cuban economy and the need for reform. In a 2007 speech he discussed inadequate salaries, inefficient domestic production, and the need for structural changes (Sullivan 2011). The government began to implement a series of reforms focused on increasing individual consumer rights and improving economic productivity.

Starting in 2008, the government began to relax restrictions on the sale of private property, allowing Cuban citizens to sell personal computers, cellphones, DVDs, and home appliances. Prior to this, such items had been available only through the black market. The state also relaxed prohibitions on the sale and renting of property; houses and apartments could previously be exchanged only through *permutas*, or swaps.[7] Only Cubans and permanent residents are allowed by law to buy and sell property, and they are limited to one main residence. Legislation allowing foreigners to buy property, solely in resort developments, has been pending for several years.

Large-scale reforms were undertaken in land ownership and agricultural production. In 2008, the government began permitting individuals and established cooperatives to apply for 10- and 25-year leases to exploit idle land.

---

6. Jane Bussey, "Cuba Dollar Decision a Sign of Distress," *Miami Herald*, October 28, 2004.

7. Ley 65 de 23 de diciembre de 1988, "Ley General de la Vivienda," modificada por el Decreto Ley 288 de fecha 28 de diciembre de 2011 [Law 65 of December 23, 1988, "General Housing Act," as amended by Decree Law 288 dated December 28, 2011].

Cubans working the land may now consume or sell crops and livestock.[8] The usufruct is basically a nontransferable lease and can be revoked if the land is abandoned or not worked for six months.[9] Moreover, the state still retains ownership of these lands. Cuba has also again started allowing surplus production (production in excess of the government quota) to be sold at private farmers' markets. Sellers—often middlemen who buy from farms—pay the state a 10 percent tax on total sales. By 2011, over 60 percent of Cuba's 1.9 million hectares of idle land had been distributed to private farmers (Feinberg 2011). The government also allowed farmers to increase their prices for items such as milk, meat, and vegetables (Laverty 2009). By the end of 2012, a new law on cooperatives was enacted, indicating a move away from government control over significant areas of agricultural production, services, small industries, and transportation. The legislation included mechanisms to create as well as dissolve cooperatives, offering a legal framework for their operation within the logic of a market economy. The law allows for the creation of second degree or cluster cooperatives, a legal mechanism that facilitates the coordination of activities and the establishment of stable relationships between cooperatives.

Between 2011 and 2012, the government implemented a number of reforms that gave Cubans additional freedom to engage in private market transactions. For example, in October 2011, the government authorized the sale of automobiles and the following month authorized Cubans to buy and sell real estate. Beginning in December 2011 state-run banks were given permission to extend loans to individuals, and individuals were allowed to use personal collateral to obtain loans.[10] The government also lifted the ban that had been in place for more than a decade prohibiting Cubans from staying at luxury hotels.

One of the most telling reforms was the elimination, in October 2012, of exit permits and the requirement to have a letter of invitation for travel abroad. The measure was implemented in January 2013, allowing Cubans to leave the country for up to 24 months and, equally important, return to Cuba with their rights intact. To travel, Cubans must obtain a passport and a visa, if required by the destination country. The government, however, still maintains

---

8. Decree-Law 259, published July 18, 2008, awards plots of land in usufruct for an initial period of 10 years (the original decree allowed 13.42 hectares to landless people and 40 hectares to those linked to a state farm, Basic Units of Cooperative Production [UBPC], or agricultural production cooperative; the latter was increased to 67.10 hectares in 2012).

9. The rationale for this is discussed in "Socialism Signifies Social Justice and Equality, But Equality Is Not Egalitarianism," speech by General of the Army Raúl Castro Ruz, president of the Councils of State and Ministers, during the conclusion of the First Ordinary Session of the 7th Legislature of the National Assembly of People's Power, International Conference Center, Havana, July 11, 2008, Year 50 of the Revolution.

10. Isaac Risco, "Cuba Under Raúl Castro's Reforms," *Havana Times*, February 22, 2013, www. havanatimes.org (accessed on May 6, 2013).

its authority to restrict the travel of highly trained professionals, professional athletes, and anyone else for reasons of national security.

The government remains the main source of employment, although the Castro regime has begun to lessen that role. At the end of 2009 Cuba's government payrolls boasted over 85 percent of the workforce, over 5 million people. In 2010 Castro pledged to remove 500,000 workers from state payrolls and expand the private sector to absorb these laid-off workers, bringing back the program of self-employment, authorizing individuals to open private microenterprises. The government approved 178 sectors (subsequently increased to 181) in which private employment would be allowed, ranging from carpentry to babysitting to umbrella repair to planning *quinceañera* parties. The government issued 250,000 licenses for self-employment. While the layoffs have not taken place as scheduled, Castro has pledged to put the package into place within five years. At the end of 2004, an estimated 400,000 Cubans were self-employed,[11] and between 2010 and 2013, the number of individuals working in small businesses more than doubled, from around 160,000 to 390,000. The path to implementation has not been without bumps. Cuba banned the private sale of imported goods in October 2013, a measure that affected an estimated 20,000 small businesses. News reports have recently cited difficulties obtaining licenses as well as increased oversight of license holders.[12]

In December 2012, the government authorized the creation of cooperatives in a number of areas, allowing workers to collectively open businesses or take over existing state-run businesses in areas such as restaurants, beauty salons, and barbershops, as well larger ventures in transportation and construction. This is a pilot project that the government may expand in the future. So far, incentives seem strong: As few as three people can form a cooperative, and tax rates for coops are lower than for self-employed workers. Likewise, contracts between state and nonstate sectors were liberalized, opening the possibility for improved synergies between the two. Private wholesale markets and credit mechanisms were allowed to support the emerging private sector.

While Cuba has started taking incremental steps toward enhancing the role of the market in its economy, the Guidelines for Cuban Economic and Social Policy, adopted at the Party's Sixth Congress in 2011, emphasize that "[t]he socialist planning system will continue to be the main national management tool of the national economy...[e]conomic planning will influence...the market and take into account its characteristics."[13]

---

11. Ibid.

12. Marc Frank, "Cuba Shutters Private Theaters, Threatens Other Businesses," Reuters, November 2, 2013, www.reuters.com/article/2013/11/03/us-cuba-reform-idUSBRE9A105P20131103 (accessed on November 2, 2013).

13. See General Guideline 1 under Economic Management Model at www.cuba.cu/gobierno/documentos/2011/ing/l160711i.html (accessed on January 29, 2014).

In his speech at the closing of the Ninth Ordinary Session of the National Assembly in 2012, President Raúl Castro promised the following changes affecting firms and workers:[14]

> Toward this end [gradual privatization], a group of enterprises has been selected to carry out an experiment in which they are granted sufficient autonomy and ample authority in their economic and financial management, to establish a new system of relationships between enterprises and the state. This experience, of great complexity and magnitude, will facilitate the elimination of existing obstacles to the development of productive forces in the state sector and the design, and subsequent approval, of a new law governing socialist state enterprises.... Likewise, a draft new Labor Code has been developed, with the goal of adjusting the rights and responsibilities of workers to new conditions, taking into account the incorporation of new non-state forms of economic management.

Even with the significant economic reforms carried out to date, Cuba is far from a free enterprise economy. Cuban state-owned enterprises (SOEs) provide services to the government and to other SOEs, employ a large although falling percentage of Cubans (paid in CUPs), and are an essential part of the socialist framework. In the transition to a freer market, many SOEs will need to be privatized to relieve the pressure on government coffers, generate revenue, stimulate economic growth, and reduce shortages (by now a staple characteristic of the Cuban economy).

Another complicating factor in carrying out reforms is the significant role the Cuban military plays in the economy: Estimates suggest that about 60 percent of the economy remains in the hands of military managers.[15] That said, the military has helped propel many of the economic reforms. As Frank Mora (2006, 16) writes, "the pragmatism of these officers is evidence of their steadfast commitment to finding alternative and effective means of defending and strengthening the Revolution...the survival and continuity of the regime hinges on the ability to reform and make necessary adjustments."

Also at play is the existence of a sizable informal sector. Until the fall of the Soviet Union and the end of Soviet support to Cuba, the Cuban informal economy focused on fulfilling the goods not supplied by state markets (Domínguez 2004). The price gap between informal markets and state shops was not substantial (González Gutiérrez 1997, quoted in Domínguez 2004). The special period led to falling incomes and a jump in informal sector labor activities as Cubans sought to supplement their state incomes. During the first reform period, and now since the Raúl Castro reforms, many previously illicit jobs have migrated into the informal economy. The informal economy has probably grown in the past decade, and many Cubans with official jobs

---

14. Raúl Castro, "It is imperative to overcome old habits and demand adherence to expectations and rigor as norms of our everyday conduct," *Granma Internacional*, Havana, July 25, 2012.

15. See, for example, Suchlicki (2007) and Gershman and Gutiérrez (2009).

engage in less formal activities to supplement their income. Richard Feinberg (2013) estimates that public sector employees who also engage in significant private economic activities could add up to between 10 and 20 percent of the workforce. Archibald Ritter (2005) and Ted Henken (2005) discuss the difficulties of measuring the informal economy in Cuba, which ranges from so-called legitimate underground economic activities to selling goods stolen from the state. While the Cuban informal sector is plagued by similar regulatory and legal obstacles to doing business as are found in other developing countries, it is distinguished by the fact that many private economic activities, unless explicitly licensed by the state, are considered criminal. While the exact extent of informal activity is unknown, it probably accounts for at least a quarter to a third of the economy today.

Since the collapse of the Soviet bloc, Cuba has gradually shifted its point of reference from Eastern Europe to East Asia. The experiences of China, and, to a lesser degree, Vietnam, have served as beacons for Cuba's reforms. China's market reforms, tightly guided by the Communist Party, are seen in Cuba as a successful transition with benefits that have extended to the social arena (Pérez Villanueva 2012, 25). Cuba has, in words and deeds, expressed a strong preference for a gradual approach combining measured liberalization with a continued large role for the state in a manner that would preserve jobs, education, health services, stability, and—though not stated publicly—ensure continued one-party control of the government.

In an article reflecting on German reunification, Robert Zoellick, then World Bank president, emphasized the importance of anticipating difficulties: "It is nearly impossible to predict precise incidents, but one can perceive trends and lay groundwork for contingencies."[16] This Policy Analysis aims to help US policymakers and entrepreneurs think through the issues that will form part of this groundwork.

---

16. Robert Zoellick, "Lessons of German Unification," *Huffington Post,* October 1, 2010, www.huffingtonpost.com/robert-b-zoellick/post_981_b_747116.html (accessed on June 18, 2013).

3

Cuba in the International Economy

Quite unlike insulated North Korea, Cuba has maintained ties to the international economy through a number of commercial agreements. These provide a solid basis for implementing the norms of a market economy.

Cuba was a founding member of the General Agreement on Tariffs and Trade (GATT) and remains a member in good standing in the World Trade Organization (WTO)—though close examination will be required to determine whether Cuban commercial policies conform to the WTO rulebook. Moreover, Cuba has trade and investment relations with most countries in the world and has forged bilateral partnerships and regional economic ties with most countries in Latin America and the Caribbean. For nearly two decades, Canada, the European Union, and recently China have been Cuba's top trading partners (see tables 3.1 and 3.2). Between 2000 and 2011, two-way Cuba-China trade saw the largest expansion, growing at an average compound rate of 15 percent annually.

In the realm of political economy, Cuba has been a member of the United Nations since its formation in 1945.[1] Cuba was a founding member of the Organization of American States (OAS), but its membership was suspended in 1962. Cuba currently takes part in regional integration initiatives including the Latin American Integration Association, the Association of Caribbean States (ACS), the Community of Latin American and Caribbean States (CELAC, in which Cuba assumed the presidency in 2013), and the Bolivarian Alliance for

---

1. The United Nations serves as a forum for countries to voice their opposition to the US embargo against Cuba. The year 2013 was the 22nd consecutive year in which the General Assembly adopted a resolution calling for the embargo's end by a vote of 188 to 2 (Israel and the United States). See "General Assembly renews call for end to US embargo against Cuba," UN News Centre, October 29, 2013, www.un.org (accessed on December 20, 2013).

Table 3.1 Cuban exports to top destination markets (millions of US dollars)

Country	1990	2000	2011
China	282	78	822
Canada	89	275	712
European Union	445	599	655
Venezuela	8	5	343
Guyana	5	19	95
Brazil	90	21	92
Belize	—	18	91
Ghana	1	13	65
Russia	n.a.	277	45
Switzerland	10	16	33
World	1,357	1,566	6,700

n.a. = not available

Note: A dash indicates a value less than $0.5 million.

Source: International Monetary Fund, *Direction of Trade Statistics*, 2013.

the Peoples of Our America (ALBA). To summarize, Cuba's involvement in the legal fabric of international economic and political relations has significant room to grow, but existing ties offer the roots for deeper integration.

General Agreement on Tariffs and Trade and World Trade Organization

Cuba was one of the original 23 signatories in 1947 to the GATT and joined the WTO when it was created in 1995. Cuba's bound (most favored nation) tariffs are scheduled with the WTO; accordingly, when they export to Cuba, all WTO members (including the United States) are entitled to pay no more than the most favored nation tariff. All WTO members are likewise entitled to the full range of Cuban commitments under the WTO accords. Of course the United States currently restricts trade with Cuba (availing itself, if challenged, of Article XXI, the national security exception to GATT obligations), and Cuba likewise restricts trade with the United States through government control of imports. However, WTO obligations would apply to US-Cuba trade following political normalization and congressional approval of normal commercial relations with Cuba.[2]

2. At the most recent WTO ministerial, in December 2013, Cuba, backed by Bolivia, Nicaragua, and Venezuela, held up a consensus agreement on a package of measures in an attempt to incorporate language in the trade facilitation agreement that would challenge the US embargo with

Table 3.2 Cuban imports from top source markets (millions of US dollars)

Country	1990	2000	2011
Venezuela	511	1,011	4,194
European Union	1,152	1,447	2,293
China	277	257	1,148
Brazil	93	104	605
Canada	150	229	515
Mexico	114	230	392
United States	2	3	387
Algeria	—	—	334
Vietnam	13	38	297
Russia	n.a.	89	126
World	2,956	3,808	14,300

n.a. = not available

Note: A dash indicates a value less than $0.5 million.

Source: International Monetary Fund, *Direction of Trade Statistics*, 2013.

Organization of American States

The Organization of American States (OAS) was established in 1948. Both Cuba and the United States were among the 21 founding members.[3] The United States has a history of using its political weight in international institutions, including the OAS, to influence the foreign policy of other countries toward Cuba. The OAS charter enumerates peaceful democracy as a primary objective. In January 1962, the OAS declared that Marxist-Leninist ideology is inconsistent with its principles and singled out Cuba as an offender. In July 1962, the OAS imposed a member country sanction on trade in military goods with Cuba, and further supported the US quarantine of Cuba during the Cuban Missile Crisis in October 1962. At the same time, the OAS suspended Cuba's participation in OAS meetings and affairs. Between 1964 and 1975, at US insistence, the OAS called upon its members to cease commercial relations with Cuba.[4] In 2009 the OAS voted unanimously to lift Cuba's "suspension" and agreed to allow Cuba to participate in the organization pending further

---

respect to goods in transit. Cuba reached agreement on compromise language with the United States, affirming "that the non-discrimination principle in Article V of the [General Agreement on Tariffs and Trade] GATT 1994 remains valid" and Cuba dropped its veto. See "WTO Approves Bali Package after U.S., Cuba Overcome Differences," *Inside US Trade*, December 12, 2013, www.insidetrade.com.

3. The OAS currently has 35 members.

4. Over time, most member states unilaterally eased their restrictions on trade with Cuba.

dialogue to discuss OAS principles. However, the extent of Cuba's participation remains subject to a "process of dialogue"—and to date Cuba has expressed no interest in reengaging with the OAS (Lee 2012).[5]

African, Caribbean, and Pacific Group of States and Forum of the Caribbean Group of ACP States

In 2000, Cuba was formally admitted to the African, Caribbean, and Pacific (ACP) Group of States, which includes 48 countries from sub-Saharan Africa, 16 from the Caribbean, and 15 from the Pacific. While the ACP was originally founded to facilitate aid and cooperation with the European Union, it has become an important advocacy and negotiating group for developing countries in the WTO.[6] After joining ACP, Cuba also became a member of the Forum of the Caribbean Group of ACP States (Cariforum), which coordinates policy dialogue with the European Union and promotes cooperation in the Caribbean region. Cuba's participation in these groups facilitated a "partial scope" agreement between Cuba and the Caribbean Community (Caricom) in 2000. However, Cuba is not a signatory to either the ACP-EU Cotonou Agreement (2000) or the Cariforum-EU Economic Partnership Agreement (2008).[7] This is due to the EU requirement that Cuba first take steps toward democratic governance and improved human rights. As the European Union is Cuba's largest trading partner, with nearly $3 billion in two-way goods trade in 2011, many see Cuba's accession to the ACP agreements—following some degree of political normalization—as a feasible next step for Cuba's enhanced integration on a regional and global basis. Cuba can certainly improve its human rights record consistent with a gradualist approach and perhaps implement political competition on a limited scale (e.g., for local offices). However,

---

5. One impediment to this dialogue is the OAS's Democratic Charter, adopted in 2001.

6. In a recent speech during the ACP Ministers of Trade meeting, WTO Director-General Pascal Lamy characterized the ACP members as one of the more powerful and influential negotiating arms of the WTO: "With your geographical reach and contributions of your membership, the ACP continues to play an instrumental role in moving forward the debate in Geneva.... The views of the ACP on what you consider to be the present and future priorities for the multilateral trading system are essential to making that process relevant and useful." See "Lamy cites ACP's 'instrumental role' in moving the trade debate forward," October 24, 2012, www.wto.org (accessed on April 4, 2013).

7. The Cotonou Agreement has been called the most comprehensive agreement between developing countries and the European Union. The agreement's subsequent revisions (latest 2010) aim to address key development challenges including climate change, food security, regional integration, state fragility, and aid effectiveness. The Cariforum-EU Economic Partnership Agreement (EPA) promotes sustainable development and economic integration in the Caribbean region and contains asymmetrical obligations and transition periods that allow Cariforum commitments to be phased in over time for trade in goods and services, investment, intellectual property rights, and competition policy. See European Commission, Introduction to the Cariforum-EU EPA, December 2009, http://trade.ec.europa.eu (accessed on April 5, 2013).

full democracy in the European sense of open competition for the highest offices does not currently seem compatible with the Cuban concept of gradualism.

Latin American Integration Association and Bolivarian Alliance for the Peoples of Our America

Cuba is a member of the Latin American Integration Association (Spanish acronym, ALADI). ALADI was originally established in 1960 as the Latin American Free Trade Agreement (LAFTA) by seven Latin American countries, including Argentina, Brazil, and Mexico, with the intent of forming a common market. LAFTA transitioned into ALADI through the 1980 Treaty of Montevideo, which created an organization devoted to Latin American integration. Cuba was the last country to join, in 1999, and now some 14 countries participate in ALADI. It has served as an "umbrella organization through which webs of trade and investment relationships among the members may ultimately produce, in the aggregate, an economically unified Latin America" (Backer and Molina 2009, 210). ALADI promotes economic and trade preferences in Latin America, particularly through agreements between member countries. Cuba has 18 trade agreements with both individual and groups of ALADI members. While these bilateral and regional agreements form the core of Cuba's portfolio of trade agreements, Cuba has also expanded its ties to other important trading partners, including China, through a series of economic and technical cooperation agreements and memoranda of understanding.

An outgrowth of ALADI's economic integration initiatives was the Bolivarian Alliance for the Peoples of Our America (generally referred to by its Spanish acronym, ALBA). Originally conceived as a response to the Free Trade Area of the Americas (FTAA) initiative of the 1990s, seen by Cuba and Venezuela as US-driven, ALBA has grown to include eight member countries in Latin America and the Caribbean.[8] ALBA's stated purpose is to promote Latin American integration "independent of colonial powers" and to "create a sub-regional bloc...grounded in the founding ideology of ALBA—socialist and public law oriented—for the betterment of the peoples in the member states and to serve as protection against other states or economic blocs."[9] ALBA pays rhetorical attention to alleviating poverty and the social exclusion of the underprivileged, but skeptics would argue that its central purpose is to bolster the political fortunes of regional autocrats.

A central feature of ALBA is a barter system whereby goods and services are exchanged based on a country's specialty—for example, Cuban medical personnel are exchanged for Venezuelan oil. This arrangement has increased

---

8. Members of ALBA are (in order of accession): Cuba, Venezuela, Bolivia, Nicaragua, Dominica, Antigua & Barbuda, Ecuador, and St. Vincent & the Grenadines. ALBA also has three observer countries, Haiti, Iran, and Syria.

9. For the history and objectives of ALBA, see Backer and Molina (2009).

the role of service exports in the Cuban economy, as noted in chapter 1. In particular, this arrangement has been central to Petrocaribe, an energy cooperation agreement between Venezuela and Caribbean countries, including Cuba. In October 2000, Fidel Castro and Venezuelan president Hugo Chávez signed the *Convenio Integral de Cooperación*, or comprehensive cooperation agreement, in which Venezuela agreed to provide 53,000 barrels per day of oil to Cuba in exchange for technical support in education, health care, sports, and science and technology. Between 30,000 and 50,000 Cuban doctors and other professionals have migrated to Venezuela as part of this swap. In 2005, Venezuela increased its discounted oil shipments to Cuba to 90,000 barrels per day.

Beyond trade initiatives, ALBA also created the Banco de ALBA, which provides credit to member countries and funding for so-called grandnational projects in areas such as education, trade, transportation, and tourism. These projects have had varying success. Programs like Sí, Se Puede, aimed at reducing illiteracy, the Programa Hambre Cero to address malnutrition, and telecommunication projects have been implemented successfully. Other programs have stalled, mostly due to severe mismanagement.[10] For regional transactions, ALBA seeks to expand the use of a common currency called the Sucre (Sistema Único de Compensación) as an alternative to the US dollar.[11]

Bilateral Investment Treaties

Cuba has signed 61 bilateral investment treaties (BITs) with the countries listed in table 3.3. BITs establish terms and conditions for foreign direct investment (FDI) and are an important aspect of international cooperation because (with limitations) they guarantee investors the right of establishment, national treatment, and most favored nation treatment. Most BITs include mechanisms for dispute settlement, generally under the auspices of the International Center for Settlement of Investment Disputes (housed in the World Bank)—though Cuba is currently not a member of ICSID. In general, Cuban BITs offer arbitration procedures in accordance with rules promulgated by the United Nations Commission on International Trade Law (Uncitral) or in some cases through the International Chamber of Commerce. While Cuba does not have a BIT with the United States, it has negotiated BITs with countries from every region around the world, including advanced countries such as Spain, Italy, and the United Kingdom.[12]

---

10. Joel D. Hirst, "What is the Bolivarian Alternative to the Americas and What Does It Do?" *Americas Quarterly*, May 2, 2012, www.americasquarterly.org (accessed on May 3, 2013).

11. Venezuela and Ecuador pioneered the use of the sucre as a trading currency in 2010. See ICTSD, "Ecuador y Venezuela esperan extender uso del Sucre" ["Ecuador and Venezuela are attempting to extend use of Sucre"], *Bridges Weekly* 8, no. 10, June 2011, http://ictsd.org/i/news/puentesquincenal/108365 (accessed on February 7, 2014).

12. For details on Cuba's BITs, see the investment section in chapter 7.

Table 3.3 Cuba's bilateral investment treaties (BITs)

Partner country	Date signed	Date of entry into force
Algeria	September 22, 1999	—
Argentina	November 30, 1995	June 1, 1997
Austria	May 19, 2000	November 25, 2001
Barbados	February 19, 1996	August 13, 1998
Belarus	June 8, 2000	August 16, 2001
Belgium-Luxembourg	May 19, 1998	—
Belize	April 8, 1998	April 16, 1999
Bolivia	May 6, 1995	August 23, 1998
Brazil	June 26, 1997	—
Bulgaria	December 16, 1998	May 24, 2000
Cambodia	September 26, 2001	—
Cape Verde	May 22, 1997	January 8, 2003
Chile	January 10, 1996	September 30, 2000
China	April 20, 2007	December 1, 2008
Colombia	July 16, 1994	—
Croatia	February 16, 2001	—
Denmark	February 19, 2001	—
Dominican Republic	November 15, 1999	—
Ecuador[a]	May 6, 1997	June 1, 1998
Finland	December 17, 2001	—
France	April 25, 1997	November 6, 1999
Germany	April 30, 1996	November 22, 1998
Ghana	November 2, 1999	—
Greece	June 18, 1996	October 18, 1997
Guatemala	August 20, 1999	August 10, 2002
Guyana	October 22, 1999	—
Honduras	August 9, 2001	—
Hungary	October 22, 1999	November 24, 2003
Indonesia	September 19, 1997	September 29, 1999
Italy	May 7, 1993	August 23, 1995
Jamaica	May 31, 1997	—
Laos	April 28, 1997	June 10, 1998
Lebanon	December 14, 1995	January 7, 1999
Malaysia	September 26, 1997	October 27, 1999
Mexico	May 30, 2001	March 29, 2002

(continues on next page)

Table 3.3 Cuba's bilateral investment treaties (BITs) *(continued)*

Partner country	Date signed	Date of entry into force
Mongolia	March 26, 1999	October 18, 2000
Mozambique	October 20, 2001	February 26, 2002
Namibia	June 27, 1997	—
Netherlands	November 2, 1999	November 1, 2001
Panama	January 27, 1999	May 11, 1999
Paraguay	November 21, 2000	December 6, 2002
Peru	October 10, 2000	November 25, 2001
Portugal	July 8, 1998	June 18, 1999
Qatar	November 6, 2001	—
Romania	January 27, 1996	May 22, 1997
Russia	July 7, 1993	July 8, 1996
San Marino	January 1, 2002	—
Serbia	August 28, 2000	—
Slovakia	March 22, 1997	December 5, 1997
South Africa	December 8, 1995	April 7, 1997
Spain	May 27, 1994	June 9, 1995
Suriname	January 7, 1999	—
Switzerland	June 28, 1996	November 7, 1997
Trinidad and Tobago	May 26, 1999	January 7, 2000
Turkey	December 22, 1997	October 23, 1999
Uganda	January 1, 2002	—
Ukraine	May 20, 1995	December 4, 1996
United Kingdom	January 30, 1995	May 11, 1995
Venezuela	December 11, 1996	April 15, 2004
Vietnam	October 12, 1995	October 1, 1996
Zambia	January 22, 2000	—

a. Ecuador terminated its BIT with Cuba and eight other countries in 2008.

Note: A dash indicates BIT has not entered into force.

Sources: United Nations Conference on Trade and Development, Full List of Bilateral Investment Agreements Concluded, as of June 1, 2013, http://unctad.org/Sections/dite_pcbb/docs/bits_cuba.pdf; International Centre for Settlement of Investment Disputes, 2013, https://icsid.worldbank.org/ICSID/FrontServlet?requestTyp e=ICSIDPublicationsRH&actionVal=ParticularCountry&country=ST166; Kluwer Arbitration, www.kluwerarbi-tration.com/CommonUI/BITs.aspx?country=Cuba.

Most sectors in Cuba are legally open to FDI under Law 77, except the health and education sectors and firms that service the armed forces (while the military controls large swaths of economic activity, these are not legally excluded from FDI). Yet in practice most of the legally open sectors are still closed. Despite Cuba's sizable portfolio of BITs, the number of joint ventures

Table 3.4   Joint ventures in Cuba, by country, 2011

Country	Number of joint ventures	Percent of total joint ventures in Cuba
Spain	47	19
Italy	25	10
Canada	23	9
France	14	6
Venezuela	11	4
Netherlands	6	2
United Kingdom	6	2
Germany	5	2
China	5	2
Mexico	5	2
Brazil	4	2
Russia	4	2
Chile	3	1
Panama	3	1
Israel	2	1
Other	82	33
Total	245	100

Source: Pérez Villanueva and Alejandro (2012, figure 3).

in Cuba remains small: In 2011, there were 245 joint ventures in Cuba (see table 3.4 and Feinberg 2012 for a detailed assessment of these numbers). Spain accounted for 19 percent of total projects, followed by Italy and Canada with 10 and 9 percent, respectively. In 2011, the top sectors for FDI in Cuba were tourism (40 percent), oil (10 percent), food (7 percent), and mining (4 percent) (see table 3.5).

World Intellectual Property Organization

Cuba has been a member of the World Intellectual Property Organization (WIPO) since 1975, shortly after it was created. WIPO, a subsidiary institution of the United Nations, was created to take over the work of copyright and patent conventions established more than a century ago and is tasked with protecting intellectual property worldwide. WIPO currently has 185 member states and oversees 24 international treaties, of which Cuba is a signatory of 16 (box 3.1).

Table 3.5 Total inward foreign direct investment in Cuba, by sector, 2011

Sector	Percent
Tourism	40
Other	17
Oil	10
Food industry	7
Mining	4
Beverages and spirits	3
Construction	3
Real estate	3
Construction materials	2
Energy	2
Financial banking	2
Light industry	2
Maritime transport	2
Tobacco	2
Communications	1
Total	100

Source: Pérez Villanueva and Alejandro (2012, figure 4).

Bilateral Aid Relations

While Cuba has achieved many of the United Nations' Millennium Development Goals (MDGs), various challenges continue to draw bilateral aid to Cuba. At the same time, Cuba has become a significant donor (for its size) in the health field, particularly in postdisaster aid. Cuba's work in Haiti, after the devastating earthquake of 2010, was highly visible.

Challenges in Cuba itself include a weak industrial base, low agricultural productivity, food insecurity, and high vulnerability to natural disasters. Bilateral aid is generally channeled to Cuba through national development agencies and initiatives but also comes through UN agencies including the United Nations Development Program (UNDP), the United Nations Educational, Scientific, and Cultural Organization (UNESCO), and the Food and Agriculture Organization (FAO). Cuba has formed development partnerships with countries in the Organization for Economic Cooperation and Development (OECD) including the European Union, Canada, and Japan, and emerging-market countries, foremost China. However, Cuba is not a signatory of the Paris Declaration on Aid Effectiveness of 2005, which aims to improve the quality of aid and its measurable impact on development, or the Accra Agenda for Action of 2008,

Box 3.1   WIPO treaties signed by Cuba

- The Berne Convention (Cuba joined in 1996)—a foundational agreement of WIPO dating from 1886—establishes a framework for the basic principles for minimum copyright protection granted to literary and artistic works, with special provisions regarding developing countries.

- The Budapest Treaty (1993) mandates that patent applications requiring the deposit of microorganisms must recognize any "international depositary authority"—scientific institutions capable of storing microorganisms.

- The Lisbon Agreement (1963) establishes procedural rules on the international registration of intellectual property rights and provides protections for internationally registered appellations of origin, i.e., geographical indications.

- The Locarno Agreement (1998) establishes an international classification system for the registration of industrial designs.

- The Madrid Agreement–Indications of Source (1904) prohibits the use of false or deceptive indications of source that mislead the consumer as to the origin of goods and establishes procedures for prohibiting imports or seizing such goods.

- The Madrid Agreement–Marks (1989) and Madrid Protocol (1995), respectively, do two things: (1) establish a system of international registration of trademarks and (2) amend the Madrid Agreement with provisions that offer increased flexibility and compatibility with the domestic legislation of countries unable to join the agreement.

- The Nairobi Treaty (1984) protects the Olympic symbol (five-interlaced rings) from commercial use without the authorization of the International Olympic Committee.

- The Nice Agreement (1995) establishes a system for classifying goods and services for the registration of trademarks and service marks, consisting of 34 classes for goods and 11 classes for services.

- The Paris Convention (1904)—a foundational agreement of WIPO dating from 1883—establishes substantive provisions in three areas: (1) national treatment, (2) the right of priority, and (3) common rules as related broadly to "industrial property" (now termed "intellectual property"), including patents, markets, industrial designs, utility models, trade names, geographical indications, and the repression of unfair competition.

- The Patent Cooperation Treaty (1996) establishes international patent application procedures, which enable a company to seek patent protection simultaneously in multiple countries.

- The Patent Law Treaty (2000) aims to harmonize and streamline formal procedures in national and regional patent applications, such as standardized requirements for obtaining a filing date and the implementation of electronic filing.

(continues on next page)

which aims to deepen implementation of the Paris Declaration and facilitate greater cooperation between aid donors.[13]

Net official development assistance (ODA) to Cuba was approximately $129 million in 2010 and $84 million in 2011.[14] The top ten donors of gross ODA to Cuba (averaged over 2010 and 2011) included Spain ($31 million), the European Union ($15 million), Canada ($6 million), and the United States (primarily via UN agencies, $15 million).[15] Table 3.6 shows the breakdown of bilateral ODA in Cuba by sector. In 2010–11, more than half of total ODA in Cuba was concentrated in a few categories: other social sectors (28 percent), education (11 percent), multisector (10 percent), and production (9 percent).

Similar to foreign direct investment, bilateral aid initiatives in Cuba face a constrained environment—both procedurally and politically—in which donors

---

13. OECD, Overview on Paris Declaration and Accra Agenda for Action, www.oecd.org/dac/effectiveness/parisdeclarationandaccraagendaforaction.htm (accessed on April 8, 2013).

14. According to the World Bank definition, ODA consists of concessional loans and grants by official agencies of member countries of the Development Assistance Committee (DAC), by multilateral institutions, and by non-DAC countries.

15. See OECD, Aid Statistics, Recipient Aid at a Glance, February 19, 2013, www.oecd.org/countries/cuba.

Table 3.6 Bilateral official development assistance (ODA) to Cuba, by sector, 2010–11

Sector	Percent of total ODA
Other social sectors	28
Education	11
Multisector[a]	10
Other and unallocated/unspecified	10
Production	9
Health and population	4
Economic infrastructure and services	2
Humanitarian aid	2
Program assistance	0
Action relating to debt	0

a. Multisector includes environmental policy, environment education, training, and research; urban development and management; rural development; and nonagricultural alternative development.

Source: OECD Development Assistance Committee, Aid Statistics, Cuba Recipient Aid at a Glance, www.oecd.org/dac/stats/recipientcharts.htm.

must build constructive partnerships with Cuban officials.[16] Development programs require a local partnership with an official government agency or nongovernmental organization (NGO), and approval may be required from government agencies including the Ministry of Foreign Commerce and Investment (MINCEX), Cuba's national agency for international cooperation. Donors in Cuba often must work within government development priorities in politically "nonsensitive" areas, such as agriculture, energy, environmental issues, and natural disaster recovery, while areas such as monetary and exchange rate policies, industrial and energy policies, and the telecommunication and transportation sectors are generally less accessible to Western donors (Feinberg 2011). As a result, the impact of bilateral aid is limited and, as Richard Feinberg (2011) suggests, "the overall amount of economic assistance is too small to have a macro-impact on economic growth, but at the micro-level, there is evidence that foreign assistance can make a positive difference...external donors can improve the lives of targeted beneficiaries, both by improving the quality of social services and by raising firms' productivity and incomes."

---

16. This section draws heavily from the analysis of Cuba's international development cooperation in Feinberg (2011); see his report for details of the political, procedural, and cultural constraints facing donors in Cuba.

Since 1996, the United States has provided bilateral aid—under the umbrella term "democracy assistance"—to Cuba through the US Agency for International Development (USAID) and the State Department. US aid is allocated to Cuba for the primary purposes of (1) development of independent civil society, (2) promotion of freedom of information, and (3) humanitarian assistance.[17] The United States has a large "nonembassy" staff in Havana but no official diplomatic relations, nor do other US agencies have staff on the ground in Cuba. Moreover, Cuba does not allow compliance with US democracy assistance. These facts hinder US-Cuba development cooperation. Between 1996 and 2011, the US Congress approved a total of $205 million for Cuba democracy assistance, appropriating nearly 87 percent of these funds since 2004 (GAO 2013, 10). US aid is primarily channeled through regional and international organizations and US-based, Cuba-specific NGOs, which generally provide technical and material assistance to Cuba, as well as US-based universities pursuing research on democratic transition in Cuba. Since 2008, regional and international organizations have received the majority of US funding, 74 percent, while Cuba-specific NGOs and universities received 14 and 10 percent, respectively (GAO 2013). US support for these programs has waned since the trial and imprisonment of Alan Gross, a USAID subcontractor accused of subversion against the Cuban state in 2011.

As one of Cuba's largest trading partners, the European Union has sustained a measurable amount of development assistance to Cuba. Between 1993 and 2003, the European Commission financed 145 million euros in assistance to Cuba, primarily in humanitarian aid but also in the areas of food security, cofinancing of NGOs, and economic cooperation.[18] In the wake of new sanctions, development cooperation was suspended in 2003, but the restrictions were lifted in 2008, facilitating new programs worth 50 million euros channeled through both UN agencies and European NGOs. The EU Development Cooperation Instrument (which coordinates aid granted by individual EU member states) reported that an additional 20 million euros would be allocated to Cuba for the period 2011–13 and would target three priority sectors: (1) food security (10 million euros); (2) environment and adaptation to climate change (7 million euros); and (3) expertise exchanges, training, and studies (3 million euros). However, bilateral aid programs vary widely among EU member states: While Spain, France, Germany, Switzerland, and Belgium provide development assistance, many other European nations offer little to none.

Although precise figures on China's development assistance are not available, estimates suggest that Chinese aid to Cuba could be substantial (see Lum et al. 2009). Reportedly, China has facilitated 70 development assistance projects in Cuba, including hydroelectric projects, agricultural irrigation, and

---

17. For more detail on US foreign assistance to Cuba, see GAO (2013). Table 2 in that report provides a summary of recent Cuba program assistance and target beneficiaries.

18. This section draws on European Commission (2010).

housing construction (Feinberg 2011). On a more commercial basis, China has invested in Cuban agriculture, telecommunications, and tourism sectors, while Cuba has invested in tourism and biotech in Beijing and Shanghai and has established a number of ophthalmic clinics in China (Zuo 2010). In 2008, China offered an estimated $70 million in concessional loans to Cuba for hurricane relief and hospital maintenance (Lum et al. 2009). China, through its state oil company China Petrochemical Corporation (SINOPEC), signed an agreement in 2008 with the Cuban oil firm Cubapetroleo (CUPET) to help develop potential oil resources.

4

US Sanctions against Cuba

The US embargo on Cuba has evolved over the past 50 years, expanding and contracting with successive administrations while seeking a few core goals.[1] Sanctions against Cuba to some extent impact other countries that engage in commerce with Cuba, while making exceptions for food, medicines, and humanitarian aid and preserving the core goals of promoting democracy and ending the abuse of human rights. The changing texture of sanctions reflects not only differing views of successive US presidents and the ebb and flow of human rights abuses by the Castro regime but also Cuba's evolving role in the international arena, from Soviet military ally, to proponent of revolution in Latin America, to provider of expeditionary troops in Africa, and, in the most recent installment, close ally of the Hugo Chávez regime in Venezuela.

The Fidel Castro regime came to power on January 1, 1959, and on January 7 was officially recognized by the United States. Immediately the regime set about seizing private lands and property and nationalizing private companies, including those belonging to US citizens and corporations. The United States initiated a partial embargo on Cuba in October 1960, after the Castro regime nationalized US property located in Cuba.[2]

---

1. In this chapter we provide a snapshot history and capsule description of US sanctions against Cuba. For considerably more detail, consult the Cuban case studies in Hufbauer et al. (2007), the update of these case studies on the Peterson Institute website (www.piie.com), and the many sources cited therein.

2. This was not the first US restriction on trade with Cuba. In 1958, the United States imposed an arms embargo after armed conflict broke out between the rebels and the Batista regime. In the summer of 1960, the United States cancelled its Cuban sugar quota; about the same time, Cuba and the Soviet Union signed a trade agreement in which Cuba agreed to export sugar to the Soviet Union and the Soviet Union agreed to export crude oil to Cuba. US-owned refineries in Cuba refused to process crude oil purchased from the Soviet Union.

US-Cuban diplomatic relations were severed in January 1961, and the embargo was further strengthened in February 1962, when the United States banned all imports from Cuba. At the same time, all US exports to Cuba, except medicine and food, were prohibited. Relations during the remainder of the Kennedy administration were deeply colored by the Cuban Missile Crisis of October 1962 and Cuba's enduring alliance with the Soviet Union. Over the next few years, the United States continued to sever ties by banning all travel of US citizens to Cuba, nearly all exports,[3] and Cuban trade with foreign subsidiaries of US firms.

These restrictions remained in place until 1977, when the Carter administration initiated limited commercial relations. President Jimmy Carter proposed a fishing agreement with Cuba and also loosened travel restrictions. Under the administration's guidance, US Treasury restrictions were revised to allow modest remittances from US residents to Cuban residents.

US-Cuban relations deteriorated in the early 1980s, during the Reagan administration. President Ronald Reagan sought support from other Latin American countries and reinstated the travel ban to Cuba in 1982. In 1986 the Reagan administration again strengthened the trade embargo and reduced the allowance for remittances. Not much changed under the George H. W. Bush administration: While both Castro and Bush indicated a mutual desire to improve US-Cuban relations, no significant action was taken on either side to do so, and in fact, the Cuban Democracy Act was passed at the end of Bush's term.

With the fall of the Soviet Union, Cuba faced increasingly difficult times. Large numbers of Cuban refugees attempted to enter the United States but were denied and ultimately detained at the Guantanamo Bay military base (controlled by the United States under a perpetual lease from Cuba). Increased tension between the United States and Cuba resulted in the Clinton administration further tightening controls on travel to Cuba and completely banning all remittances to Cuba. Later in 1994, Cuba and the United States reached an agreement to stem the influx of Cuban refugees. In return, the United States agreed to grant additional immigration visas to Cuban citizens. Following this show of diplomacy, President Bill Clinton eased travel restrictions to Cuba. Relaxation did not last long. After Cuba shot down two private American planes (operated by the advocacy group Brothers to the Rescue), Congress passed the restrictive Helms-Burton Act. Throughout the remainder of the Clinton administration, the United States attempted to cast an anti-Castro spell in international arenas but faced pushback from many countries as well as repeated UN condemnations of the US embargo. The tide shifted somewhat near the end of President Clinton's second term as Congress passed the Trade Sanctions Reform and Export Enhancement Act in the fall of 2000, which allowed one-year licenses for the export of US goods to Cuba.

---

3. Food and medicine exports were banned in 1964 when the US Commerce Department revoked export licenses. However, humanitarian donations to nongovernmental organizations operating in Cuba were generally allowed.

When President George W. Bush took office in 2001, he instructed the US Treasury to augment the Office of Foreign Assets Control in order to better enforce sanctions against Cuba. The following year, the Bush administration created the Initiative for a New Cuba, which was designed to reach out to Cuban citizens and deliver humanitarian assistance through nongovernmental organizations. In 2003, in response to human rights violations, President Bush again tightened sanctions and the next year continued with democracy-building initiatives. Throughout its tenure, the George W. Bush administration remained confrontational in relations with Cuba.

The Obama administration initiated a major policy shift in US-Cuban relations. In the spring of 2009, shortly after taking office, President Barack Obama repealed standing restrictions on travel to Cuba and allowed US citizens to once again send remittances to their Cuban relatives. President Obama initiated a dialogue with Cuba regarding legal immigration of Cubans to the United States. Cuba was receptive and, in September 2009, the Obama administration further eased restrictions on travel and remittances to Cuba in order to promote contact between separated relatives.[4] Over the last four years, Cuba has cooperated to a greater extent with international organizations and has modestly moved toward democratic norms even as it has continued human rights abuses and taking political prisoners.

Major Legislation

In this section we describe the major legislative acts that shape commercial relations with Cuba. We do not describe the multiple and extensive executive orders that carry out congressional instructions. Suffice it to observe that enabling legislation gives the president a great deal of latitude to tighten or relax the sanctions regime toward Cuba.

Trading with the Enemy Act, 1917

The Trading with the Enemy Act (TWEA) was enacted in the midst of World War I, enabling the president to invoke almost unlimited trade and financial restrictions, and property seizures, with respect to countries deemed hostile

---

4. Much has been made of the handshake between Presidents Obama and Raúl Castro in South Africa at the memorial service for Nelson Mandela in December 2013. The White House made statements downplaying the handshake, but statements by both leaders indicate some warming. President Obama, at a fundraiser in Miami on November 8, 2013, suggested that it may be time to revise policies toward Cuba. President Castro addressed relations with the United States in a speech on December 21, 2013: "If we really want to move forward in our bilateral relations, we have to learn to mutually respect our differences and become accustomed to peacefully living with them." See Marc Frank, "Cuba president notes tone of recent relations with U.S.," Reuters, December 21, 2013, www.reuters.com/article/2013/12/21/us-cuba-usa-raulcastro-idUS-BRE9BK0E820131221.

to the United States.[5] Until the passage of the International Emergency Economic Powers Act (IEEPA) in 1977, the TWEA provided the statutory basis for nearly all sanctions invoked by the United States. The TWEA was initially invoked against Cuba in July 1963, in order to freeze all Cuban assets in the United States. As of 2008, Cuba was the only country still subject to sanctions under the TWEA.

Foreign Assistance Act, 1961

The Foreign Assistance Act of 1961 reorganized US mechanisms for delivering foreign aid. The Act bars assistance to any government that engages in human rights violations. Congress included an amendment prohibiting assistance to governments that provide aid to Cuba so long as the Castro regime remains in power.

Proclamation 3447, 1962

In February 1962, President John F. Kennedy issued Proclamation 3447, which established an embargo on all trade between the United States and Cuba. The embargo included the importation of all goods of Cuban origin, as well as goods imported into the United States from or through Cuba. In addition, all exports from the United States to Cuba were prohibited. The proclamation also gave the secretaries of the Treasury and Commerce the authority to carry out the embargo and establish exceptions to the embargo, "by license or otherwise, as he determines to be consistent with the effective operation of the embargo."[6]

Cuban Assets Control Regulations, 1963

The Cuban Assets Control Regulations (CACR) (31 CFR Part 515) were announced by the US Treasury Department's Office of Foreign Assets Control (OFAC) in 1963. The CACR were issued under the authority of TWEA and is the primary regulatory regime under which the embargo against Cuba is implemented (Propst 2011). The CACR prohibit not only the import and export of goods between the United States and Cuba but also transactions related to property, including investment, financial, trade, and travel-related transactions. These restrictions apply to all individuals and entities subject to US jurisdiction, as well as persons engaged in transactions that involve property

---

5. The president must declare a "national emergency" in order to invoke the powers of the TWEA, but such a declaration is completely discretionary.

6. The American Presidency Project, "Proclamation 3447—Embargo on All Trade with Cuba," John F. Kennedy Proclamation, February 7, 1962, www.presidency.ucsb.edu/ws/index.php?pid=58824 (accessed on April 15, 2013).

subject to US jurisdiction. The CACR prohibit four categories of transactions with Cuba:

1. Travel
   - Travel to Cuba by any person subject to US jurisdiction, unless they obtain authorization through a license.
2. Financial transactions
   - The transfer of credit and payments between, by, through, or to any banking institution subject to US jurisdiction or by any individual subject to US jurisdiction.
   - All transactions in foreign exchange by any person subject to US jurisdiction with Cuba, including the exportation of gold, silver, bullion, currency, or securities.[7]
   - Transactions with respect to securities registered in the name of a Cuban national.
3. Transactions involving property
   - The transfer, withdrawal, or export of any property that Cuba or Cuban nationals, wherever located, have any interest in.
   - All transfers outside the United States and any property subject to US jurisdiction.
4. Transactions involving merchandise trade
   - The purchase, transport, or import of merchandise that is of Cuban origin, has been transported through Cuba, or is made or derived from any article produced or manufactured in Cuba.

Export Administration Act, 1979

The Export Administration Act (EAA) (15 CFR § 746) regulates US exports to Cuba. The EAA prohibits the United States from exporting goods to countries that have been designated sponsors of terrorism. In 1982, Cuba was designated a sponsor of terrorism and was effectively cut off from US goods. Under the EAA, the Export Administration Regulations (EAR) prohibit the export or reexport of US-origin goods, software, and technology to Cuba, unless the exporter is authorized to do so through a license or specific exception. Exports that require a license are "subject to a general policy of denial," except in the case

---

7. The CACR do, however, permit remittances to Cuban nationals. Persons subject to US jurisdiction are authorized to make periodic remittances to individuals, provided that total remittances do not exceed $500 in any consecutive three-month period and are not made from a blocked source. The CACR also allow licensed travelers to carry remittances of up to $3,000 and allow a one-time emigration-related remittance of $1,000. In 2004, periodic remittances were reduced from $500 to $300 and were restricted to members of the remitter's immediate family. However, in 2009, the Obama administration restored the rules on remittances as outlined in the CACR.

of certain goods that may be considered more favorably for export approval.[8] These include

- medicines and medical devices,
- items necessary to provide efficient and adequate telecommunications links between the United States and Cuba, including links established through third countries,
- exports from third countries of nonstrategic, foreign-made items that contain an unsubstantial portion of US-origin material (less than 20 percent),
- exports intended to provide support for the Cuban people (e.g., commodities for human rights organizations that promote independent activity and strengthen civil society, such as computers and printers), and
- aircraft that temporarily stop in Cuba to deliver humanitarian goods or services.

Additionally the EAR list 13 license exceptions that allow export and reexport without a license. These include, among others, software updates and replacement parts for legally exported commodities, humanitarian donations, and items in transit from Canada through the United States.[9]

Cuban Democracy Act, 1992

The Cuban Democracy Act, named because it was intended to promote a peaceful transition from the Castro regime to democracy, was passed in 1992. Under the premise that the Castro regime violated "internationally accepted standards of human rights," the Act prohibits foreign-based subsidiaries of US companies from dealing with Cuba and US citizens from traveling to Cuba or sending remittances to Cuba. Further, the Cuban Democracy Act allows the president to terminate aid to any country that provides assistance to Cuba. The Act clearly differentiates between the Castro regime and citizens of Cuba, calling for increased support for the Cuban people in the form of exports of medical supplies and donations of food to nongovernmental institutions. Finally, the Cuban Democracy Act allows telecommunications between the United States and Cuba, enables direct mail service between the United States and Cuba, and permits assistance on a case-by-case basis.

---

8. See 15 CFR § 746.2, www.ecfr.gov/cgi-bin/text-idx?c=ecfr&SID=9ae4a21068f2bd41d4a5aee843 b63ef1&rgn=div5&view=text&node=15:2.1.3.4.30&idno=15#15:2.1.3.4.30.0.1.2.

9. For a complete list, see 15 CFR § 746.2, www.ecfr.gov/cgi-bin/text-idx?c=ecfr&SID=9ae4a21068f2 bd41d4a5aee843b63ef1&rgn=div5&view=text&node=15:2.1.3.4.30&idno=15#15:2.1.3.4.30.0.1.2.

Helms-Burton Act, 1996

The Helms-Burton Act, also known as the Cuban Liberty and Democratic Solidarity Act of 1996, strengthened the US embargo against Cuba. The Act was originally introduced in 1995, tabled, and reintroduced in February 1996 after Cuban fighter jets shot down two private planes operated by a Cuban refugee advocacy group called Brothers to the Rescue. This context is relevant given the Act's intention to initiate a peaceful transition to a representative democracy and market economy in Cuba.

Titles I and II of the Helms-Burton Act, respectively, codified the US embargo on trade and declared the US policy goal to facilitate the transition to a democratic government in Cuba. Title I contains a provision allowing the president to waive the embargo, in whole or part. The Helms-Burton Act identified Cuba's confiscation of US property in Cuba as theft. Title III permits Americans to sue foreign entities that traffic in confiscated US property; however, the president has the authority to waive Title III for successive periods of six months (and has done this since Helms-Burton was enacted). Title IV requires the United States to deny access to individuals who are involved in transactions related to the trafficked property described in Title III. Additionally, under Title IV, the United States is prohibited from providing aid to countries that provide military or intelligence support or assistance to Cuba.

The Helms-Burton statute contains a tough list of conditions that should be met before the US president can waive the restrictions on Cuban trade and investment. A "transition government" must be in place before the restrictions can be lifted, and the definition of that government lists the conditions. See box 4.1 for the relevant language.

It must be recognized that there are as many "political" as "legal" constraints on presidential action. In the first place, no statute can override the president's inherent authority over the conduct of foreign affairs under Article II of the US Constitution—an authority that has been liberally interpreted by the courts.[10] Second, American political tempers may well change once the Castro brothers no longer control Cuba's destiny, making it easier for the president to interpret Helms-Burton strictures in a relaxed fashion.

Both points are illustrated by the way President Clinton and the Congress handled the Jackson-Vanik Amendment in 2000, when the time came to vote on permanent normal trade relations (PNTR) with China. PNTR was the legal prelude for mutual recognition, by China and the United States, of their respective rights and responsibilities once China joined the World Trade Organization (which it did in 2001). Recall that the Jackson-Vanik Amendment to the Trade Act of 1974 prohibited normal trade relations, export credits, or investment guarantees to any "nonmarket economy" country

---

10. The Supreme Court spoke favorably of "the generally accepted view that foreign policy [is] the province and responsibility of the Executive" in *Department of the Navy v. Egan*, 484 U.S. 518, at 529 (1988). For a detailed analysis, see Powell (1999).

Box 4.1   Section 205 of the Helms-Burton Act: Requirements and factors for determining a transition government

(a) REQUIREMENTS - For the purposes of this Act, a transition government in Cuba is a government that

(1) has legalized all political activity;

(2) has released all political prisoners and allowed for investigations of Cuban prisons by appropriate international human rights organizations;

(3) has dissolved the present Department of State Security in the Cuban Ministry of the Interior, including the Committees for the Defense of the Revolution and the Rapid Response Brigades;

(4) has made public commitments to organizing free and fair elections for a new government

(A) to be held in a timely manner within a period not to exceed 18 months after the transition government assumes power;

(B) with the participation of multiple independent political parties that have full access to the media on an equal basis, including (in the case of radio, television, or other telecommunications media) in terms of allotments of time for such access and the times of day such allotments are given; and

(C) to be conducted under the supervision of internationally recognized observers, such as the Organization of American States, the United Nations, and other election monitors.

(5) has ceased any interference with Radio Marti or Television Marti broadcasts;

(6) makes public commitments to and is making demonstrable progress in

(A) establishing an independent judiciary;

(B) respecting internationally recognized human rights and basic freedoms as set forth in the Universal Declaration of Human Rights, to which Cuba is a signatory nation; and

(C) allowing the establishment of independent trade unions as set forth in conventions 87 and 98 of the International Labor Organization, and allowing the establishment of independent social, economic, and political associations.

(7) does not include Fidel Castro or Raúl Castro; and

(8) has given adequate assurances that it will allow the speedy and efficient distribution of assistance to the Cuban people.

(b) ADDITIONAL FACTORS - In addition to the requirements in subsection (a), in determining whether a transition government in Cuba is in power, the President shall take into account the extent to which that government

(1) is demonstrably in transition from a communist totalitarian dictatorship to representative democracy;

(2) has made public commitments to and is making demonstrable progress in:

(A) effectively guaranteeing the rights of free speech and freedom of the press, including granting permits to privately owned media and telecommunications companies to operate in Cuba;

(continues on next page)

(code for communist country) that, among other measures, "denies its citizens the right or opportunity to emigrate...." When PNTR was enacted in 2000, as today, China had an established practice of denying assorted "troublemakers" the right to emigrate by the simple expedient of denying them a passport.[11] At the time, however, Congress was far more concerned about Chinese trade practices than a spotty human rights record, and notwithstanding the amendment, Chinese restrictions on emigration were not a big factor in the public debate.

No president will want to lift trade and investment restrictions against Cuba if he or she faces strong congressional opposition. Quite possibly, as political relations enter a more normal phase, the president will seek congressional repeal (or significant modification) of the Helms-Burton statute before lifting sanctions. But it is also possible, once political normalization is under way, that the president will be able to waive some sanctions under a relaxed interpretation of Helms-Burton conditions, even without seeking legislative approval.

Trade Sanction Reform and Export Enhancement Act, 2000

This Act was passed in 2000, during the last months of the Clinton administration. It did not affect US imports from Cuba but rather created exceptions for exports to Cuba. The Act enabled the president to grant one-year export licenses for food and medical shipments to Cuba. Additionally, it established a specific license for business travel related to the newly permitted export exceptions. The Act required that all transactions be paid in advance, either in cash or through foreign banking institutions.

---

11. See Andrew Jacobs, "No Exit: China Uses Passports as Political Cudgel," *New York Times*, February 22, 2013, www.nytimes.com (accessed on May 30, 2013).

Recent Reforms

Since President Obama took office in 2009, the US government has undertaken a number of reforms to "bridge the gap among divided Cuban families and promote the freer flow of information and humanitarian items to the Cuban people."[12] Several amendments to the CACR were implemented between 2009 and 2012. Below we describe some of the main reforms.

2009 Amendment

In 2009, OFAC loosened the restrictions on travel, allowing Americans to visit close relatives in Cuba. The definition of "close relatives" was broadened to include "any individual related to a person by blood, marriage or adoption who is no more than three generations removed."[13] OFAC also dropped the one visit per year limitation and increased the per diem limit on living expenses in Cuba and the per-trip limit on transportation-related expenses. Rules related to family remittances were amended by eliminating the limit on the dollar amount and the frequency of family remittances to Cuban nationals, increasing the dollar amount and frequency of emigration-related remittances, and increasing the dollar amount of remittances that authorized travelers may carry to Cuba.[14] Restrictions on certain telecommunication services, contracts, related payments, and travel-related transactions were somewhat eased to allow travel for telecommunication service providers and to allow professionals to attend meetings related to commercial telecommunications (Sullivan 2012a).

2010 Amendment

In 2010, OFAC authorized the export from the United States or from outside the United States, by persons subject to US jurisdiction, of certain services used in the exchange of personal communications over the internet (e.g., email, instant messaging, blogging, and web browsing).

2011 Amendment

In 2011, OFAC loosened restrictions on travel to Cuba for educational purposes, by allowing accredited US academic institutions to engage in travel to Cuba. Prior to the amendment only full-time permanent employees and students could travel to Cuba, through their accredited academic institution. As amended,

---

12. White House, Office of the Press Secretary, "Fact sheet: Reaching out to the Cuban people," www.whitehouse.gov/the_press_office/Fact-Sheet-Reaching-out-to-the-Cuban-people (accessed on April 18, 2013).

13. *Federal Register* 4600, "Rules and Regulations," volume 74, no. 172, www.treasury.gov.

14. For more details, see Sullivan (2012a, 4–6 and 20–21).

15 CFR allows all faculty members and staff to engage in travel through any sponsoring US academic institution. The CACR were also amended to include "people-to-people" exchanges: Licenses are granted for educational exchanges not associated with academic study pursuant to a degree program, so long as the exchange takes place through an organization that sponsors a program to promote people-to-people contact. OFAC also loosened restrictions on remittances to support the development of private businesses (up to $500 per quarter) and unlimited remittances for religious organizations in Cuba.

2012 Amendment

In 2012, the CACR were further amended to authorize the processing of funds transfers for the operating expenses or other official business of third-country diplomatic or consular missions in Cuba. Certain payments for services rendered by Cuba to US aircraft (e.g., payments in connection with overflights to Cuba or emergency landings in Cuba) are now permitted. Prior to the amendment, such payments required a specific license.

Myanmar Is No Precedent

Fresh in mind today is the relatively rapid political and economic transition in Myanmar. In 2012, the Obama administration, along with several US allies, decided to try a new recipe to achieve a degree of political liberalization in a country long run by the military autocracy, most notable for keeping opposition leader Aung San Suu Kyi under house arrest since 2003.[15] Around the same time, Myanmar's leaders came to realize two geopolitical facts: Without liberalization, their country would become a pariah within the Association of Southeast Asian Nations; and without opening to the West, their country would increasingly resemble a Chinese satellite.

The new Obama recipe emphasized carrots rather than sticks, and the taste test started with Secretary Hillary Clinton's publicized visit to Rangoon, with a photogenic embrace of Aung San Suu Kyi, on November 30, 2011. Building on quiet diplomacy, Myanmar's military leaders agreed to hold partly free elections and allow Aung San Suu Kyi to travel abroad and play a political role at home; in exchange, the United States, Japan, the European Union, and others lifted, in whole or part, their trade and financial bans and even encouraged their multinational corporations to invest in Myanmar. Since Japan and Europe were quicker to liberalize, some US firms now feel disadvantaged in the new Myanmar; yet step by step the United States is dismantling its array of barriers to doing business. Economic relations were moving toward normal footing by the end of 2013, just 13 months after Clinton's visit.

---

15. Aung San Suu Kyi was also put under house arrest between 1989 and 1995 and from 2000 to 2002.

Some observers may view Myanmar's transition from pariah to semi-normalization as a template for Cuba. However, the differences between US economic relations with Myanmar and those with Cuba are immense:

- Myanmar and the United States are far apart in every economic dimension: distance, language, trade, investment, and tourism. By contrast, Cuba and the United States are potentially very close.

- Even with complete normalization, US two-way merchandise trade with Myanmar will not exceed $1.6 billion annually, and the stock of US foreign direct investment (FDI) in Myanmar is not likely to surpass $1 billion for many years. By contrast, following complete normalization, US two-way merchandise trade with Cuba could exceed $10 billion annually and US FDI stock could soon reach $2 billion, given the right framework for economic transactions.

- While US two-way services trade with Myanmar is not likely to reach $500 million annually, two-way services trade with Cuba could easily exceed $2.5 billion annually—again with the right framework.

- As the caveats suggest, the United States did not have a deep backlog of economic issues to resolve with Myanmar, once political normalization was under way. By sharp contrast, there are few if any countries where the US backlog of economic issues is longer than with Cuba.

- Finally, and perhaps most important, while it is worrying to the United States when Myanmar's leaders are corrupt and traffic in drugs, if these same national characteristics become prominent in Cuba that will deeply distress not only the US government but all Americans.[16]

In light of these differences, we do not see the rapid normalization of US economic relations with Myanmar as a plausible template for economic normalization with Cuba. With new leadership in Havana, political normalization could happen quickly, but thorny issues need to be hammered out in the economic space. The right way to think about economic normalization is akin to a trade agreement with friendly partners that have significant differences in their economic systems. For example, President George W. Bush launched the talks for the Central American Free Trade Agreement–Dominican Republic (CAFTA-DR) in January 2002, and after ratification by all participants, the agreement entered into force in January 2009, a time span of seven years.[17] Full economic normalization with Cuba could take even longer.

---

16. To be sure, the United States was not particularly concerned about Cuban corruption or drugs during the Batista regime in the 1950s. But that was a different era, long before Mexican drugs, violence, and corruption became front page news in the American press.

17. The Dominican Republic did not enter the talks until 2004.

The key reason is that the commercial concessions the United States will want from Cuba far exceed what the United States has asked of Myanmar—and are also significantly greater than what the United States asked of its CAFTA-DR partners. In reciprocity terms, the US leverage for securing meaningful liberalization of the Cuban market for imported goods and services and foreign investment will be opening the US market for Cuban firms that want to sell and invest in the United States. To achieve a balanced commercial relationship with Cuba, it will be crucial for the United States *not* to open its markets unilaterally before the Cuban government extends appropriate and reciprocal concessions to US firms and workers and agrees to procedures that ensure effective implementation. Negotiating this bargain will be difficult and could take several years before a package is ready for congressional consideration.

5

Initial Steps to Normalization

A half century of separation has diminished commerce between the United States and Cuba to a trickle. Political normalization, when it happens, will open the door to economic normalization. Our thesis, however, is that the door should be opened carefully and in both directions. It would be a mistake for the United States to throw the door wide open for Cuban exports, if Cuba continues to control the flow of goods and services imports from the United States and limits the opportunities for US firms to invest. Competitors based in Canada, Mexico, Europe, and elsewhere have long since established a semblance of normal economic relations with Cuba—to the extent consistent with a state-controlled socialist economy. There is no reason for US firms and workers to be permanently left behind when the new day dawns. In this chapter we walk through issues and sectors that should be ripe for normalization—on a reciprocal basis—when the time comes to negotiate the economic agenda.

Some scholars may argue that unconditional US withdrawal of sanctions and the complete opening of US markets to Cuban merchandise, services, and investment offer the fastest path forward for Cuban economic progress. We disagree, for two reasons. First, we believe that Cuba's embrace of *all* tenets of a market economy can best ensure rapid growth—as happened in the Baltic states and Poland after the end of the Cold War and Soviet control. Second, past experience shows that rent seeking is deeply embedded in the great majority of economies that are emerging from a socialist past. As a rule, vested interests strongly resist the reduction of tariff and nontariff barriers to foreign competition, oppose foreign investment, and protest the adoption of modern intellectual property laws and commercial codes. Reciprocal negotiation can tilt the political economy balance in favor of liberalization—because certain firms and workers in the transition country grasp the immediate benefit to themselves of reducing barriers that protect the home market. This has been the European Union's experience in its extensive network of association agreements. It was also the US experience with the North American Free Trade Agreement (NAFTA), the Central American Free Trade Agreement–Dominican Republic (CAFTA-DR), and bilateral free trade agreement negotiations with Morocco, Korea, Peru, Colombia, and many others. We believe that the same reciprocal arithmetic—well before the United States and Cuba contemplate a free trade agreement—offers the most certain path toward Cuban liberalization. With this background in mind, we turn to practical steps.

Heeding former US Trade Representative (USTR) Robert Zoellick's exhortation to anticipate the transition, the US government should begin to engage the Cuban government in specific steps to liberalize trade that fall short of lifting sanctions but would help create a climate of Cuban opinion favoring a market economy and fostering entrepreneurs with a stake in positive US-Cuba economic relations. The Council of the Americas Task Force on Cuba identified a number of measures that could be undertaken without congressional approval. Several could be implemented as part of an "early harvest" to reward Cuba if the government implements economic reforms that encourage private enterprise, paving the way for US companies to resume regular business activities on the island once normalization has taken place. These include[1]

- expanding the list of exceptions for trade with businesses and individuals engaged in certifiably independent economic activity. This would reward Cuba's move toward a market system and create opportunities for Cubans who are not working with state-owned enterprises or the military. Helping this group should enlarge the constituency with a stake in the market economy;

- expanding US travel licenses to include US executives. This would allow US firms to establish business ties, regardless of whether the transition is big bang or gradual;

- expanding travel licenses for Americans engaged in real estate, land titling, and financial services. This could be a reciprocal move if Cuba loosens restrictions on real estate; and

- allowing the sale of telecom hardware (cell towers, satellite dishes, and handsets) in response to Cuban relaxations, with the argument that better communications will foster more democratic forms of government.

World Trade Organization and Most Favored Nation Status

Cuba was one of the original 23 signatories in 1947 to the General Agreement on Tariffs and Trade (GATT) and (unlike its relations with the International Monetary Fund and World Bank) has continuously remained a member in

---

1. The measures listed here are the most promising among those suggested in Council of the Americas and Americas Society (2013).

good standing in the GATT and subsequently the World Trade Organization (WTO). Cuba has scheduled its bound tariffs with the WTO (table 5.1) and, in accordance with the most favored nation (MFN) principle, exports from the United States to Cuba are entitled to these and all other Cuban commitments under the WTO. Of course, under current circumstances, the United States is limiting exports to food and medicine, but once political relations are normalized, US exports should—in principle—enjoy the same access to the Cuban market as exports of all other countries.

Cuban exports to the United States are more problematic.[2] Under the Jackson-Vanik Amendment to the Trade Act of 1974, products exported from "nonmarket" countries that restrict the freedom of emigration and otherwise violate human rights are not eligible for MFN access to the US market.[3] Instead, those goods must pay the prohibitive duties imposed by the Smoot-Hawley Tariff of 1930. While the Jackson-Vanik Amendment was originally aimed at the Soviet Union, it has affected exports from many other "nonmarket" (meaning communist) countries.

Over the past four decades, successive US presidents have either waived the amendment on an annual basis or issued a semiannual report certifying that targeted communist countries have adopted more liberal economic policies, paid greater respect to human rights, and no longer thwarted emigration. Countries were then declared not to be in violation and were finally "graduated" to permanent normal trade relations (PNTR) through a congressional vote soon after they joined the GATT or WTO. The most recent PNTR bill, with respect to Russia, was favorably voted by Congress in 2012, but not before a searching congressional debate.[4] Much the same happened in 2000, on the eve of China's membership in the WTO. As happened with Russia and China, PNTR for Cuba will trigger a major congressional debate centered both on economic restrictions and human rights abuses. Even before PNTR, it seems likely that the president will waive the Jackson-Vanik Amendment with respect to Cuba, so it is worth looking at the congressional role in waiver determinations.

The key elements for a waiver are (1) conclusion of a bilateral trade agreement, containing a reciprocal grant of MFN status and approval by a congressional joint resolution,[5] and (2) compliance with the freedom-of-emigration

---

2. This section is based on Pregelj (2005).

3. In addition to unfavorable market access to the United States, the Jackson-Vanik Amendment restricts access to US government financial facilities and prohibits target countries from concluding a free trade agreement with the United States.

4. The congressional debate centered on the precise terms of the Magnitsky Amendment, named for a Russian lawyer tortured and killed by the Russian government for his persistence in exposing official corruption.

5. The joint resolution is voted under "fast-track" authority under Section 151 of the Trade Act of 1974. Note that a bilateral trade agreement under this section covers much less ground than a normal free trade agreement.

Table 5.1   Cuban tariff profile

Product group	Final bound duties[a]			MFN applied duties[b]	
	Average	Duty-free (percent)	Binding (percent)	Average	Duty-free (percent)
Animal products	39.6	1.1	100	9.7	2.2
Dairy products	40.0	0.0	100	22.1	0.0
Fruits, vegetables, and plants	39.2	0.8	100	9.4	5.0
Coffee and tea	40.0	0.0	100	20.5	0.0
Cereals and preparations	36.8	0.0	100	11.2	5.1
Oilseeds, fats, and oils	36.1	0.0	100	8.2	2.7
Sugars and confectionary	40.0	0.0	100	20.3	0.0
Beverages and tobacco	39.7	0.0	100	23.4	0.0
Cotton	16.0	60.0	100	1.6	60.0
Other agricultural products	33.0	15.4	100	6.3	30.8
Fish and fish products	5.1	7.1	12.2	4.7	50.8
Minerals and metals	4.1	35.1	10.4	7.7	8.0
Petroleum	3.0	0.0	80.0	2.4	20.0
Chemicals	6.5	15.8	13.0	9.5	3.0
Wood and paper	4.3	35.3	13.4	8.7	14.2
Textiles	17.7	19.6	9.0	14.6	2.0
Clothing	42.6	0.0	3.4	22.8	0.0
Leather and footwear	8.1	0.0	6.7	12.0	2.1
Nonelectrical machinery	8.7	0.3	61.8	9.7	0.8
Electrical machinery	10.8	0.0	63.4	10.4	0.0
Transport equipment	7.7	0.0	22.8	9.1	6.7
Manufactures, nes	15.5	0.0	17.0	12.5	3.6

MFN = most favored nation; nes = not elsewhere specified; HS = Harmonized System

a. For final bound duties:
Average = simple average of final bound duties excluding unbound tariff lines.
Duty-free = share of duty-free HS 6-digit subheadings in the total number of subheadings in the product group.
Binding = share of HS 6-digit subheadings containing at least one bound tariff line.

b. For MFN applied duties:
Average = simple average of MFN applied duties.
Duty-free = share of duty-free HS 6-digit subheadings in the total number of subheadings in the product group.

Source: World Trade Organization Statistics Database, 2013, http://stat.wto.org.

requirements of the Jackson-Vanik Amendment. The latter requirement can be fulfilled either by a presidential report to Congress that the country is in full compliance with the freedom-of-emigration criterion or by a presidential waiver of compliance (perhaps with specific conditions). The presidential determination of full compliance is subject to congressional *disapproval* by a joint resolution of the House and the Senate (again, a specific fast-track procedure is laid out in Section 152 of the Trade Act of 1974).

To summarize, Congress can override a presidential determination of full compliance and thus revoke an annual waiver of the Jackson-Vanik Amendment, and Congress must vote approval of PNTR to establish permanent US commercial relations with Cuba on an MFN basis.[6] What this means in practice is that, once the Helms-Burton law is waived by a presidential finding, Congress should ideally approve (or at least not disapprove) the establishment of normal commerce with Cuba.[7]

That brings us to the conclusion of a bilateral trade agreement—*not* a free trade agreement, just a basic trade agreement. In the next chapter, we offer estimates of bilateral commerce likely to result from the establishment of basic trade relations. The relevant precedents for this undertaking are the bilateral agreements between the United States on the one hand and Vietnam and Russia on the other, prior to their respective accessions to the WTO (in 2007 and 2012). Unlike Vietnam and Russia, however, Cuba is already a member of the WTO, so there will be no WTO Working Party that reviews all of Cuba's trade practices and requires significant reforms. Instead, it will be solely up to the United States to ensure that Cuba is living up to its existing WTO commitments and to negotiate reforms in Cuba's tariff and nontariff barriers. As table 5.1 shows, Cuba's bound tariffs, while high, are not out of line with the bound tariff schedules of many developing countries. Accordingly, it seems likely that most of the US negotiating effort in the bilateral trade agreement will be devoted to a multitude of nontariff barriers, starting with the fact that the Cuban government is the dominant importer of goods and services.

Reciprocity Measures

Once the Helms-Burton law is waived by a presidential finding, Congress should approve the establishment of normal commerce with Cuba, on reciprocal terms negotiated by the USTR in close consultation with Congress. A first step in the negotiating process would be for the United States to expand the list of goods that US firms can sell to Cuba. The United States and Cuba should identify tariffs and nontariff barriers that could be lowered or eliminated vis-à-vis each other's products. The parties would then conclude a bilateral trade agreement, containing a reciprocal grant of MFN treatment. On the US side, this would need to be approved by a congressional joint resolution.

---

6. Scholars might question whether these provisions are consistent with US obligations under the WTO since Cuba is a member and theoretically entitled to MFN treatment from the United States. While the question has never been litigated, if US practice were challenged, the United States would likely invoke GATT Article XXI Security Exceptions.

7. Section 204 of the Helms-Burton Act, titled "Termination of the Economic Embargo of Cuba," gives the president the authority to "take steps to suspend the economic embargo of Cuba" upon submitting a determination that a "transition government in Cuba is in power." Additionally, upon submitting a determination that a "democratically elected government in Cuba is in power," the president has the authority to "take steps to terminate the economic embargo of Cuba" (see Cuba Liberty and Democratic Solidarity [Libertad] Act of 1996 at www.gpo.gov).

Pleasure and Medical Tourism

Tourism is already big business in Cuba, and it will get much bigger with normalization. In fact, tourist destinations in the Caribbean—from the Bahamas to Barbados—dread the day when Cuba can compete on equal terms for the American tourist dollar. This dread has likely grown with the recent announcement that, after five decades, the Cuban government has lifted its ban on golf, once considered an elitist sport.[8] The British firm Esencia has received approval for the construction of a luxury golf resort in Varadero. Construction is planned to begin in 2014. Moreover, there are reportedly plans for additional projects by Chinese, Canadian, Spanish, Vietnamese, and Russian investors.[9] The Cuban government has also in principle agreed to allow foreigners to buy property within these resorts, opening up the possibility that foreigners could purchase vacation or retirement homes—undoubtedly a welcome development for Canadian snowbirds.

American tourists spend approximately $6.4 billion annually in the Caribbean, but very little in Cuba.[10] According to available statistics, Cuba's annual earnings from tourists of all nationalities were approximately $2.4 billion in 2010 (medical tourism still remains small, generating around $40 million annually [KPMG International 2011]). By comparison, Puerto Rico (population 3.7 million versus 11.3 million Cubans) earned $3.6 billion from foreign tourism in 2010.

US and Cuban restrictions on bilateral tourism are severe. Of course, given the vast differences in population size and per capita income,[11] US restrictions have far greater economic clout than Cuban restrictions. US travel to Cuba is restricted through a licensing program operated by the US Treasury's Office of Foreign Assets Control (OFAC). US citizens and permanent residents may travel under (1) a general license or (2) a specific license. The general license lists nine categories under which a US citizen or permanent resident may travel to Cuba:

1. persons visiting "close relatives" who are Cuban nationals,[12]

---

8. The market for golf tourism is significant. HSBC (2012) estimates that there are about 80 million golfers in the world and the global golf tourism market is worth $1 billion.

9. Sarah Rainsford, "Cuba golf project gets green light," BBC, May 13, 2013, www.bbc.co.uk/news/world-latin-america-22507776.

10. This figure is according to the US Bureau of Economic Analysis estimates of total US travel expenditure (travel payments excluding passenger fares) to the Caribbean in 2012 (data from International Transactions Database, www.bea.gov/iTable/index_ita.cfm).

11. The US population is 314 million, and approximately 22 million Americans go abroad annually for pleasure tourism (US Department of Commerce 2011). By contrast, the Cuban population is 11 million, and just 250,000 Cubans traveled abroad in 2010 (see World Bank, *World Development Indicators*, http://databank.worldbank.org/data/views/reports/tableview.aspx). US per capita GDP is $50,000, while Cuban per capita GDP is probably below $6,000.

12. "Close relative" is defined by the US Treasury as "any individual related to a person by blood, marriage, or adoption who is no more than three generations removed from that person."

2. persons visiting "close relatives" who are US government employees,

3. officials of the US and foreign governments or intergovernmental organizations of which the United States is a member,

4. journalists and support personnel,

5. full-time professionals conducting research or attending professional meetings,

6. faculty, staff, and students of accredited US postsecondary institutions,

7. members and staff of US religious organizations,

8. employees of US telecommunication service providers, and

9. employees of a producer or distributor of agricultural commodities, medicine, or medical devices.

OFAC issues a specific license on a case-by-case basis to persons not covered by a general license. The categories for a specific license cover persons participating in

1. educational activities,

2. support for the Cuban people (e.g., human rights organizations),

3. humanitarian projects,

4. freelance journalism,

5. professional research or meetings not covered under the general license,

6. public performances, workshops, athletic competitions, etc.,

7. activities of private foundations, research or educational institutes,

8. activities related to trade in information or informational materials,

9. activities related to exports to Cuba, and

10. visits with "close relatives" who are not Cuban nationals or US government employees.

People-to-people programs under these licensing categories have loosened the restrictions on Americans visiting Cuba. According to Emilio Morales (2013), the number of non-Cuban American visitors increased from 41,000 in 2007 to 103,000 in 2012. Over the same period, the number of Cuban-American visitors increased from 204,000 to 476,000.[13]

Cuba has entered into joint venture arrangements with major hotel and resort chains based in Europe and Canada. For example, Spain's Meliá, Grupo Barceló, and Grupo Ibero Star are some of the largest foreign-operated hotel chains in Cuba. Typically the financial arrangements call for 50-50 joint ventures, and the foreign partner has operating control. However, employment at foreign companies is controlled by the Cuban government. State-run

---

13. According to Morales (2013), the number of European visitors to Cuba declined from 671,000 in 2007 to 577,000 in 2011, as the Great Recession took its toll.

employment agencies are in charge of hiring and managing employees, as well as setting wages and paying employees (Feinberg 2012). Foreign investors pay wages to the state agency in hard currency, while the state agency pays local workers in Cuban pesos.

The global medical tourism industry was worth over $70 billion in 2010 and is expected to grow at an annual rate of 20 to 30 percent (KPMG International 2011). Deloitte (2008, 14) found that US spending on outbound medical tourism was $2.1 billion in 2008 and was projected to reach about $16 billion in 2012.

Under its sanctions regime, the United States limits travel to Cuba both by type of traveler and by dollar expenditures. As outlined above, US citizens or permanent residents can travel to Cuba for selected work, education, or religious activities. The US government also places restrictions on travel-related financial transactions. In general, persons authorized to travel to Cuba may engage in financial transactions related to travel to and from Cuba, as well as expenditures related to travel within Cuba such as hotel accommodation, meals, and personal items. However, financial transactions related to travel within Cuba may not exceed a per diem rate of $140. US citizens or permanent residents traveling under a specific license may also be subject to restrictions on transactions related to the licensed activity. Financial transactions unrelated to travel or licensed activities are prohibited; this includes elective medical services.[14]

Once travel relations are normalized, it will be easy for any American who pays for his own medical care, or who has private insurance that reimburses medical tourism abroad, to take advantage of Cuban clinics. Medicare and Medicaid are different propositions. In general, Medicare does not currently reimburse medical expenses incurred abroad.[15] Some private insurance companies have begun to explore the options of covering medical procedures and costs incurred abroad. In March 2008, Blue Shield and Blue Cross signed agreements with seven foreign hospitals, in Costa Rica, Ireland, Thailand, Turkey, and Singapore.[16] The hospitals are accredited by Joint Commission International, a US nongovernmental organization that offers accreditation and certification of hospitals, primary care, clinical, and other medical services in the United

---

14. Exceptions are permitted for the purchase of recorded music, publications, and expenditures related to telecommunication services.

15. Medicare will pay for healthcare services in a foreign hospital under three situations: (1) the closest hospital available for the treatment of a medical emergency is in a foreign country; (2) the closest hospital available for the treatment of a medical emergency while traveling from Alaska to another US state via Canada is in Canada; and (3) the closest hospital available for treatment of a particular medical condition, regardless of whether it is a medical emergency, is in a foreign country.

16. Bruce Einhorn, "Medical Travel Is Going to Be Part of the Solution," *Bloomberg Businessweek*, March 17, 2008, www.businessweek.com (accessed on March 12, 2013).

States and overseas.[17] Medicaid, for people of limited means, is jointly funded by the federal government and the states. Consequently, any use of Medicaid assistance abroad would require both state and federal authorization. If and when the United States discovers medical tourism as one answer to the inflated cost of health care, it seems unlikely that Cuba would be the first beneficiary of liberalized Medicare and Medicaid rules. Mexico seems more likely, along with other US partners in free trade agreements. However, given the strong ethnic ties between Cuba and certain states (particularly Florida and New Jersey), its proximity, and abundance of highly skilled doctors, Cuba is a likely beneficiary of a second wave of liberalization.

Reciprocity Measures

When US sanctions are lifted, American citizens will be able to travel freely to Cuba to enjoy tourism activities. At the same time, Cuba should take steps to ensure that US tourism firms have the same standing in Cuba as do Canadian, Spanish, Chinese, and other companies for investing through joint ventures and wholly foreign-owned enterprises and for bidding on government contracts. The United States could further encourage trade by fostering medical tourism, capitalizing on Cuba's strength in medical services. With appropriate certification of Cuban facilities, and with permission for US health firms to invest in Cuba, the US Congress might permit the Department of Health and Human Services to authorize Cuban hospitals and clinics to provide Medicare and Medicaid services.

International Monetary Fund, World Bank, and Inter-American Development Bank[18]

Following political normalization, Cuban membership in international financial institutions (IFIs)—the International Monetary Fund (IMF), the World Bank, and the Inter-American Development Bank (IADB)—would seem to be an early step in the process of economic normalization. Cuban membership would open the door to grants, loans, and technical assistance, all badly needed to establish a functioning economy. None of this will happen without US approval.

Cuba was an original member of the IMF in 1944 (and hence a member of the World Bank) but withdrew from the Fund in 1964, shortly before a meeting of the executive directors, which was called to consider whether Cuba was no longer eligible for Fund loans on account of its arrears and other short-

---

17. Participation in Joint Commission International's accreditation and certification program is voluntary. However, accreditation is recognized as an industry standard. The Joint Commission has accredited over 15,000 healthcare organizations in the United States, and its international arm, the Joint Commission International, accredits healthcare facilities in 90 countries worldwide.

18. This section is largely based on Feinberg (2011).

comings. Withdrawal from the Fund would have automatically triggered withdrawal from the World Bank, by virtue of the Bank's Articles, but in fact Cuba withdrew from the Bank earlier, in 1960. While Cuba has not since reapplied for Fund and Bank membership, in June 2011, Richard Feinberg (2011) elicited the following statement from a senior official in the Cuban Ministry of Foreign Affairs: "Cuba has no principled position against relations with the IMF or World Bank."

Whatever may be Cuba's "principled position," the US Congress has resolutely expressed its objections. Among other laws, the Helms-Burton Act of 1996 instructs the US executive directors in the IFIs "to oppose the admission of Cuba as a member of such institution until the President submits a determination that a democratically elected government in Cuba is in power." If any IFI approves a loan or other assistance to Cuba over the opposition of the United States, then the Treasury is directed to withhold an equivalent amount of money from its obligations to that IFI.

While the United States lacks the voting power to block Cuban membership in the IFIs or assistance to Cuba (a simple majority can approve such actions), in our view, other IFI members are not about to override the United States on such a sensitive matter. Nor are IFI executive directors likely to engage in Feinberg's (2011) cleverly crafted end runs around congressional objections. Without the active support of the US president and at least the passive assent of Congress, the IMF and the World Bank will remain, at an official level, strangers to Cuban economic development.

At a less formal level, however, many World Bank and IMF officials have visited Cuba over the past two decades to attend economic conferences and similar events. Among the professional IFI staff these visits have fostered considerable familiarity with economic developments in Cuba.

A similar story applies to Cuba's nonrelations with the IADB. The IADB was created in 1959, after the Cuban revolution, in large part to preclude a "second Cuba" in Latin America. Cuba was never a member. IADB membership is conditioned on membership in the Organization of American States (OAS), a body created in 1948 that can trace its lineage (through the Pan American Union) back to 1890.[19] While Cuba was at the beginning and remains to this day a *member* of the OAS, it was excluded from *participation* in OAS activities by a vote of the members in 1962. In 2009, the OAS unanimously rescinded that exclusion. However, the extent of Cuba's participation remains subject to a "process of dialogue" (Lee 2012), because, officially at least, Cuba characterizes the OAS as "an imperialist organization."[20] So, despite some confusion on this

---

19. In the mind of Secretary of State George Marshall, a major purpose of the OAS was to fight communism in the Western Hemisphere. Cuba's exclusion from the IADB echoed this purpose.

20. During a meeting in 2012 of the Bolivarian Alliance for the Peoples of Our America (ALBA), Cuban Foreign Minister Bruno Rodríguez Parrilla specifically called the OAS "an organisation that has served to promote domination, occupation and aggression...and a platform for the US to attack

point, it is not lack of OAS membership that separates Cuba from the IADB. Rather, as with the Fund and the Bank, it is a combination of disdain by Cuba and US opposition.

The IFIs are not the only potential sources of financial assistance to Cuba. During the Cold War, the Soviet Union was a major source, providing around $250 million annually (Hufbauer, Schott, and Elliott 1990). In recent years, Europe, Canada, and other Western countries have together provided about $100 million annually to Cuba (Feinberg 2011). In July 2012, China pledged financial aid to Cuba, an undisclosed but possibly large amount, given China's aid record in Africa. But to reconstitute its economy, Cuba may well need financial assistance of billions of dollars, not hundred millions. The only plausible source of such sums, and essential technical assistance that comes with them, will be the IFIs. And the IFIs will not join the Cuban reconstruction party without a green light from the White House.

Reciprocity Measures

In order for Cuba to become a member of the IFIs, the Cuban government will need to request membership. With congressional consent, the United States should support this petition, or at least not block it—essentially the same approach the United States took in the case of the OAS.

Sugar Exports

Sugar was historically the dominant crop in Cuba's economy and the main source of foreign exchange. However, while production figures are difficult to verify, the sugarcane crop has dramatically declined, from a reported 82 million metric tons (MT) in 1990, to half that amount in the mid-1990s, to only 12 million MT in 2007, after the industry was seriously downsized. Current production levels are around 15 million MT a year.[21] A revived Cuban sugar industry, aided by foreign capital and production techniques, could play an important role in stimulating the Cuban economy, particularly with a view to the production of sugar-based ethanol, which Cuba produced during the Second World War but suspended thereafter.

Recently the Cuban sugar industry has shown signs of reform. The Communist Party's 6th Congress Policy Development Guidelines make specific reference to reviving the sugar industry. Two of the stated objectives were "increasing and sustaining the production of sugar cane" and "generating

---

and plunder Latin America and the Caribbean." See "Cuba eyes Americas Summit place, but not OAS return," BBC News, February 15, 2012, www.bbc.co.uk/news/world-latin-america-17053827 (accessed on September 17, 2013). Cuban officials even had a rhyming Spanish slogan to denigrate the OAS: Con OEA o sin OEA ganaremos la pelea [with or without the OAS we will win the fight].

21. Data accessed through the Food and Agriculture Organization FAOSTAT database, http://faostat.fao.org/site/339/default.aspx.

hard currency income to finance the total cost of operations, investments and repairs."[22] The following year, the government shut down the Ministry of Sugar, which had (mis)managed the country's sugar industry since 1964, when the ministry was established. In its place the government created a state holding company, Grupo Empresarial de la Agroindustria Azucarera—or Azcuba—comprising 13 provincial sugar enterprises with 61 sugar mills.[23] Azcuba was charged with managing production and creating "a business system capable of turning its exports into hard currency to finance its own expenses."[24]

In 2012, Cuba opened its sugar industry to foreign investment for the first time since the industry was nationalized in 1959.[25] Azcuba signed a joint management contract with Brazilian powerhouse Odebrecht's subsidiary Companhia de Obras e Infraestrutura (COI). Under the agreement, COI will manage the 5 de Septiembre sugar mill in Cienfuegos province for the next 13 years and invest in mechanized agriculture and industrial processing technologies. Azcuba also entered into a joint venture with the United Kingdom's Havana Energy to construct a biomass power plant.

Once the world's largest sugar exporter, Cuba currently exports very little sugar.[26] In the 2011–12 crop year, Cuba exported just 670,000 MT of raw sugar. China is the largest export market for Cuban sugar, followed by some European and Central Asian countries (Italy, France, Netherlands, Russia, Poland, Belarus, and Kazakhstan), and some countries in the Middle East and North Africa region (Egypt and Algeria).

Once relations with the United States are normalized, Cuba could potentially expand its exports to North America. However, Cuban exports will face large hurdles. The domestic US sugar market is protected through a system of tariff-rate quotas (TRQs) that regulate the import of raw cane sugar and refined sugar, and it is unlikely that Cuba would be able to regain its historic sugar quota. The United States allows 1,117,195 metric tons raw value (MTRV) annually of raw cane sugar and at least 22,000 MTRV of refined sugar.[27] Additionally the United States allows a maximum of 64,709 MTRV

22. Sheyla Delago Guerra, Juan Varela Pérez, and Anneris Ivette Leyva, "Cuba reorganizes sugar industry," *Granma Internacional*, December 8, 2011, www.granma.cu (accessed on March 15, 2013).

23. Azcuba is in charge of managing sugar production. Regulatory affairs and policy development related to the sugar industry were assigned to the Ministries of Agriculture and of Economy and Planning.

24. Peter Orsi, "Cuba does away with emblematic Ministry of Sugar," Associated Press, September 29, 2011, www.finance.yahoo.com (accessed on March 15, 2013).

25. Foreign direct investment (FDI) in the sugar industry has been permitted in principle since 1995, when the Foreign Investment Act was passed. However, until 2012, FDI was limited to a small number of joint ventures in the production of sugar derivative products.

26. At the time of the Cuban revolution, Cuba accounted for about one-third of global sugar exports, with the United States purchasing 60 percent of Cuban exports (Echevarría 1995).

27. These minimum levels were agreed in the Uruguay Round Agreement on Agriculture and can

of products containing over 10 percent (by dry weight) of sugars derived from sugarcane or sugarbeets. TRQs are allocated to countries based on historical exports to the United States, in consultation with those quota-holding countries. The TRQ for refined sugar is allocated primarily to Canada and Mexico and then to other countries on a first-come, first-served basis. Table 5.2 lists the raw sugar TRQs for 2013. Under the TRQ system sugar importers pay either an in-quota tariff rate of 0.625 cents per pound for raw sugar or an over-quota tariff rate of 15.36 cents per pound for raw sugar and 16.12 cents per pound for refined sugar. The United States waives these tariffs through just three pieces of legislation: (1) the Generalized System of Preferences; (2) the Caribbean Basin Initiative; and (3) selected free trade agreements.[28] For the most part, imported sugar above the TRQ levels pays the tariff when it enters the US market.

The TRQ system entails a major derogation from the spirit of WTO rules (especially GATT Article XI) but enjoys enormous political support both in the United States and among the quota-holding countries. The current world price of raw sugar is around 18 cents per pound, while the current US price is 23 cents per pound. This means that each pound of sugar that enters the US market within the TRQ system is advantaged by 5 cents, or a 28 percent price premium. The benefit adds up to $100 per ton of imported TRQ sugar. At one time, Cuba's sugar quota was 2.9 million tons, the largest of any country, before it was eliminated in 1960. The current quota-holding countries obviously will fight against any reallocation of their existing quotas to Cuba. At the same time, the US sugar industry will staunchly oppose any increase of the overall TRQ level to accommodate Cuba, since that could depress the price of sugar within the United States or require budget outlays—politically very unpopular—to support the high US price. Despite these obstacles, with the right concessions from Cuba, a way might be found for Cuba to regain some of its erstwhile sugar quota.

One option for Cuba would be to access the US market through the Caribbean Basin Initiative (CBI), which provides Caribbean economies duty-free access to the US market for certain goods. Duty-free treatment is extended to sugar, syrups, and molasses under section 2703 of the Caribbean Basin

---

be modified by the USTR if domestic supply is insufficient to meet domestic demand at reasonable prices. However, the quantity cannot fall below the minimum set by the WTO Agreement on Agriculture. The 2008 Farm Bill stated that the TRQ must be set at the minimum level required to comply with obligations under the Uruguay Round agreement.

28. The following free trade agreements (FTAs) provide a TRQ for sugar and sugar products if the FTA partner has a trade surplus in these goods: CAFTA-DR, Chile, Colombia, Morocco, Panama, and Peru. The size of the FTA partners' TRQ is the lesser of (1) the country's global trade surplus in the relevant good or (2) the quantity specified in the FTA for that year (this is published annually by USTR in the *Federal Register*).

Table 5.2   US sugar tariff-rate quota (TRQ), 2013

Country	Raw cane sugar TRQ (metric tons raw value)	Share of total in-quota TRQ (percent)
Total raw cane sugar TRQ	1,117,195	100.0
Dominican Republic	188,908	16.9
Brazil	155,634	13.9
Philippines	144,901	13.0
Australia	89,087	8.0
Guatemala	51,520	4.6
Argentina	46,154	4.1
Peru	44,007	3.9
Panama	31,127	2.8
El Salvador	27,907	2.5
Colombia	25,760	2.3
South Africa	24,687	2.2
Nicaragua	22,540	2.0
Swaziland	17,174	1.5
Costa Rica	16,100	1.4
Thailand	15,027	1.3
Mozambique	13,953	1.2
Guyana	12,880	1.2
Mauritius	12,880	1.2
Zimbabwe	12,880	1.2
Belize	11,807	1.1
Ecuador	11,807	1.1
Jamaica	11,807	1.1
Honduras	10,733	1.0
Malawi	10,733	1.0
Fiji	9,660	0.9
Bolivia	8,587	0.8
India	8,587	0.8
Barbados	7,513	0.7
Trinidad and Tobago	7,513	0.7
Congo	7,258	0.6
Côte d'Ivoire	7,258	0.6
Gabon	7,258	0.6
Haiti	7,258	0.6

(continues on next page)

Table 5.2 US sugar tariff-rate quota (TRQ), 2013
(continued)

Country	Raw cane sugar TRQ (metric tons raw value)	Share of total in-quota TRQ (percent)
Madagascar	7,258	0.6
Papua New Guinea	7,258	0.6
Paraguay	7,258	0.6
St. Kitts and Nevis	7,258	0.6
Uruguay	7,258	0.6

Source: Office of the United States Trade Representative, 2012, www.ustr.gov.

Economic Recovery Act (CBERA).[29] In order to receive duty-free access, products must

1. be imported directly from a CBI beneficiary country into the United States;

2. be wholly the growth, product, or manufacture of a CBI beneficiary country or substantially transformed into a new or different article in the CBI beneficiary country; or

3. contain a minimum of 35 percent local content of one or more CBI beneficiary countries.[30]

In addition, to be designated a CBI beneficiary country Cuba would have to meet certain mandatory and discretionary requirements. The mandatory requirements articulated under CBERA include, among others, having a democratically elected government, providing equitable market access treatment to the United States by ensuring any preferential treatment given to another developed country is awarded also to the United States, taking steps to resolve any claims regarding the expropriation or nationalization of property of US citizens, and taking steps to afford internationally recognized workers' rights to domestic workers.[31]

Another avenue by which Cuba could gain market access is through one of the US Sugar Re-Export Programs. Under these programs raw sugar can enter the United States without the application of a TRQ, provided that the sugar is used in one of the following ways: (1) refined and reexported; (2) refined and reexported in a sugar-containing product; or (3) used to produce polyhydric

29. Although the CBI waives the in-quota duty for sugar imports by the United States, the over-quota duty remains and therefore the quota is binding.

30. 15 percent of the minimum content may be from the United States (USTR 2011).

31. See chapter 1 for a discussion of expropriation issues and chapter 7 for a brief discussion of the labor issues relevant to Cuba.

alcohol.[32] These programs are intended to mitigate the effects of quotas by allowing US manufacturers to "replace" sugar in the domestic market that has been exported as refined sugar or sugar products.

Cuba could also focus on exporting sugar derivatives such as ethanol. Cuba has the land capacity to produce 70 million MT of sugarcane, which translates into 28 million MT of sugar, assuming the current area under cultivation is unchanged (Patiño 2009). This would make Cuba one of the most productive sugarcane producers in the world and if channeled into ethanol production could yield 616 million gallons of ethanol, or $1 billion in sales. Geographic proximity to large markets like the United States and the European Union, relative to other large-scale producers like Brazil, gives Cuba a market advantage. Additionally, sugar-based ethanol is more cost efficient than starch-based ethanol (e.g., from corn). The United States recently implemented domestic reforms that improve market access for foreign producers. In 2012, the United States allowed its long-standing import tariff on ethanol (54 cents per gallon) to expire and eliminated the 45 cents per gallon volumetric ethanol excise tax credit (VEETC) given to domestic ethanol blenders. Japan, Canada, and India have also expressed interest in increasing ethanol imports. To be a competitive ethanol exporter, however, Cuba will require substantial foreign direct investment to provide the financing and technology necessary to boost sugar production and develop the domestic ethanol industry. In this regard, Brazil's COI has expressed its interest in producing ethanol as well as sugarcane and signaled its intention to build a distillery at the sugar mill it jointly manages with Azcuba.[33]

Reciprocity Measures

In exchange for gaining access to the US sugar market, Cuba should implement reforms in its own agricultural sector to provide greater market access for US goods. The United States currently supplies Cuba with roughly one-third of its food and agricultural imports. However, the Cuban government places restrictions on imports that impede the ability of US producers to diversify their exports and increase their market share. As an example, the Cuban government determines the variety and quantity of imports based on unmet dietary needs (e.g., protein and carbohydrates), rather than consumer demand. Additionally, US exporters negotiate procurement contracts through the government agency Alimport instead of with the end-users of agricultural products (FAS/USDA 2008). As a result, US producers are not able to market their products based on consumer demand and cannot diversify their exports, which consist mainly of corn, soybeans, wheat, and poultry. US agricultural

---

32. US Department of Agriculture, "Sugar Re-Export Programs," www.fas.usda.gov/itp/imports/sugar/sugarreexport.asp (accessed on March 26, 2013).

33. Esteban Israel, "Brazil to breathe life into faded Cuban sugar sector," Reuters, www.reuters.com/article/2012/01/30/brazil-cuba-sugar-idAFL2E8CUA7620120130 (accessed on March 26, 2013).

producers including the National Farmers' Union, the American Soybean Association, and the National Pork Producers, among others, have advocated increasing agricultural trade with Cuba, which is considered to be a reliable trade partner with no issues related to corruption.[34] To facilitate trade, and in exchange for access to the US sugar market, Cuba should implement reforms to allow US exporters to work directly with end-users and remove restrictions on the variety of products that may be imported.

34. See FAS/USDA (2008) and National Farmers' Union, U.S.-Cuba Policy, testimony of NFU President Roger Johnson to the House Ways and Means Committee, Washington, April 29, 2010, http://waysandmeans.house.gov/media/pdf/111/2010apr29_johnson_submission.pdf.

6

Potential Commerce with the United States: Starting from a Low Base

The United States and Cuba have had limited economic ties ever since the US commercial, economic, and financial embargo on Cuba was enacted in October 1960. Over the past six years, US merchandise exports to Cuba have generally ranged between $350 million and $500 million annually, mostly foodstuffs (table 6.2).[1] US merchandise imports are practically zero. Recent loosening of a few restrictions, including the Obama administration's authorization in April 2009 for US telecommunication companies to donate equipment and establish roaming agreements with Cuban providers, has spurred some US companies to think about future investment opportunities. In addition to telecommunications and the hotel and tourism sector, where foreign investment from other countries abounds and where US companies have already expressed robust interest, several sectors offer interesting potential for US companies to do business in Cuba: energy and natural resources, agribusiness, and biotechnology.

Forecasting Trade and Investment

To project the level of bilateral commerce with normalized relations between the United States and Cuba, we employ foremost a gravity model, supplemented by a few bilateral comparisons for foreign direct investment (FDI).[2]

---

1. See also Sullivan (2013). Emilio Morales and Joseph Scarpaci (2013) claim that US gift packages (in-kind remittances) amounted to $2.5 billion in 2012. Manuel Orozco (2012) estimates that US cash remittances were around $1.3 billion in 2011, but Morales and Scarpaci (2013) contend that the figure reached $2.6 billion in 2012.

2. The gravity model analysis underlying this chapter was carried out by Dean DeRosa.

The gravity model takes into account multiple forces that determine economic ties between partners. In recent years the model has become the "workhorse" of international trade analysis (Eichengreen and Irwin 1998).

The gravity model has its origins in early quantitative studies of international trade by Jan Tinbergen (1962) and Pentti Pöyhönen (1963), who found that bilateral trade flows are strongly positively correlated with the levels of output (GDP) in partner countries and strongly negatively correlated with the distance between trading partners. Through the years, a number of geographic and political factors that augment or hinder international trade and investment have been added to these "gravitational forces." Additional explanatory variables attempt to account for other possible "natural" causes of trade, which include common borders, the same language, a shared colonial relationship, land area, access to seaports, and joint membership in preferential trading arrangements (Rose 2004). Theoretical underpinnings for the gravity model have been established by James Anderson (1979), J. H. Bergstrand (1985), Alan Deardorff (1998), and James Anderson and Eric van Wincoop (2003), among others. For this analysis, we rely on the model developed by Dean DeRosa (2007, 2009) and updated in 2012. This model has been used in a number of Peterson Institute studies of the prospective trade and investment impacts of US and other free trade agreements (FTAs).

A recurring problem in gravity model analysis is the issue of missing variables. In much of the Peterson Institute's work, DeRosa has followed Andrew Rose's (2004) approach of using pooled ordinary least squares (OLS) and controlling for year effects (such as changes in the business cycle, oil shocks, etc.) in estimating parameters. However, for the US-Cuba analysis DeRosa used the two-stage least squares (2SLS) approach, without year effects. This instrumental variable method attempts to control for possible simultaneity between the dependent variable (log bilateral trade) and two prominent gravity model explanatory variables: log joint GDP, measured in purchasing power parity (PPP) terms, and joint GDP per capita, also measured in PPP terms.[3] While 2SLS is unusual in gravity model studies,[4] it is often used in trade demand studies.[5] The 2SLS approach without year effects assumes that omitted variables—those that may affect bilateral trade flows but are not specified—do not significantly bias the estimates for the variables that are included in the present gravity model (table 6.1).

The DeRosa model is broadly similar to others but is distinguished by several important features. It is applied not only to merchandise trade but also

---

3. The instruments for the (assumed) endogenous real GDP variables are the contemporaneous product of population levels in partner countries, one-year lagged value of the product of real GDP levels in partner countries, and one-year lagged value of the product of GDP per capita levels in partner countries.

4. However, Stata software has no problem implementing the 2SLS method using gravity model data.

5. For example, for an overview of the early literature, see Goldstein and Khan (1985).

Table 6.1 **Two-stage least squares gravity model estimates for aggregate merchandise trade (SITC 0-9) and aggregate trade in services (all categories), specifying major customs unions and free trade agreements and dropping bilateral trade less than $10 million in 2008 US dollars, using data for 2000–08**

Variable		Log real merchandise trade	Log real trade in services
Log distance	Estimate	−0.735***	−0.599***
	(s.e.)	(0.021)	(0.030)
	(t-statistic)	(−34.394)	(−20.144)
Log product real GDP	Estimate	0.867***	0.811***
	(s.e.)	(0.029)	(0.029)
	(t-statistic)	(29.645)	(28.047)
Log product real GDP per capita	Estimate	−0.116***	0.056*
	(s.e.)	(0.029)	(0.033)
	(t-statistic)	(−4.017)	(1.682)
Common language	Estimate	0.239***	0.629***
	(s.e.)	(0.038)	(0.064)
	(t-statistic)	(6.221)	(9.891)
Land border	Estimate	0.627***	0.653***
	(s.e.)	(0.065)	(0.095)
	(t-statistic)	(9.707)	(6.909)
Number landlocked	Estimate	−0.080***	0.076*
	(s.e.)	(0.028)	(0.042)
	(t-statistic)	(−2.875)	(1.781)
Number islands	Estimate	0.238***	0.217***
	(s.e.)	(0.036)	(0.062)
	(t-statistic)	(6.548)	(3.494)
Log product land area	Estimate	−0.083***	−0.109***
	(s.e.)	(0.015)	(0.016)
	(t-statistic)	(−5.505)	(−6.658)
Common colonizer	Estimate	0.891***	1.533***
	(s.e.)	(0.069)	(0.224)
	(t-statistic)	(12.908)	(6.851)
Currently colonized	Estimate	−1.095***	−2.556***
	(s.e.)	(0.417)	(0.460)
	(t-statistic)	(−2.625)	(−5.551)
Ever colony	Estimate	0.553***	0.788***
	(s.e.)	(0.078)	(0.087)
	(t-statistic)	(7.074)	(9.085)

(continues on next page)

to services trade. Data on bilateral merchandise trade are compiled for just over 200 countries from the UN Comtrade dataset, using trade data under Revision 2 of the Standard International Trade Classification system (SITC). Data on bilateral services trade are compiled from the Organization for Economic Cooperation and Development (OECD) database and are necessarily limited

Table 6.1 Two-stage least squares gravity model estimates for aggregate merchandise trade (SITC 0-9) and aggregate trade in services (all categories), specifying major customs unions and free trade agreements and dropping bilateral trade less than $10 million in 2008 US dollars, using data for 2000–08 *(continued)*

Variable		Log real merchandise trade	Log real trade in services
Common country	Estimate	0.000	0.000
	(s.e.)	(0.000)	(0.000)
	(t-statistic)	(.)	(.)
GSP	Estimate	−0.268***	0.030
	(s.e.)	(0.028)	(0.045)
	(t-statistic)	(−9.512)	(0.668)
European Union	Estimate	0.320***	0.243***
	(s.e.)	(0.050)	(0.059)
	(t-statistic)	(6.441)	(4.087)
European Free Trade Area	Estimate	0.068	0.052
	(s.e.)	(0.096)	(0.118)
	(t-statistic)	(0.709)	(0.438)
EU FTAs	Estimate	0.008	−0.148***
	(s.e.)	(0.046)	(0.052)
	(t-statistic)	(0.184)	(−2.863)
NAFTA	Estimate	1.372***	0.312**
	(s.e.)	(0.156)	(0.134)
	(t-statistic)	(8.778)	(2.330)
Mercosur	Estimate	0.129	0.000
	(s.e.)	(0.237)	(0.000)
	(t-statistic)	(0.543)	(.)
CMAS FTAs	Estimate	0.528***	0.963***
	(s.e.)	(0.139)	(0.227)
	(t-statistic)	(3.809)	(4.240)
AFTA	Estimate	1.214***	0.000
	(s.e.)	(0.183)	(0.000)
	(t-statistic)	(6.652)	(.)
SAPTA	Estimate	−1.208***	0.000
	(s.e.)	(0.363)	(0.000)
	(t-statistic)	(−3.331)	(.)
Other FTAs	Estimate	0.630***	0.112
	(s.e.)	(0.064)	(0.106)
	(t-statistic)	(9.881)	(1.063)
Constant	Estimate	−16.140***	−18.025***
	(s.e.)	(0.673)	(0.792)
	(t-statistic)	(−23.999)	(−22.770)

(continues on next page)

Table 6.1   Two-stage least squares gravity model estimates for aggregate merchandise trade (SITC 0-9) and aggregate trade in services (all categories), specifying major customs unions and free trade agreements and dropping bilateral trade less than $10 million in 2008 US dollars, using data for 2000-08 *(continued)*

Variable	Log real merchandise trade	Log real trade in services
Observations	60,000	19,655
R-squared	0.657	0.656
Adjusted R-squared	0.657	0.656
RMSE	1.125	1.033
F-statistic	...	...
Number of clusters	8,769	3,276

SITC = Standard International Trade Classification; s.e. = standard error; RMSE = root mean square error; GSP = Generalized System of Preferences

Notes: Gravity model estimates using two-stage least squares with robust standard errors determined by clustering ordered country pairs. Dependent variable is log real bilateral trade, T_{ij} (country i exports to importing country j). Instruments for the (assumed) endogenous real GDP variables are the contemporaneous product of population levels in partner countries, one-year lagged value of the product of real GDP levels in partner countries, and one-year lagged value of the product of GDP per capita levels in partner countries. *,**,*** denote statistical significance at the 10, 5, and 1 percent levels, respectively. Trade agreements represented by indicator variables are European Union (EU), European Free Trade Area (EFTA), EU bilateral free trade agreements (EU FTAs), North American Free Trade Agreement (NAFTA), Southern Common Market (Mercosur), Chile, Mexico, Australia, and Singapore bilateral free trade agreements (CMAS FTAs), ASEAN Free Trade Area (AFTA), SAARC Preferential Trading Arrangement (SAPTA), and all other customs unions and free trade agreements (Other FTAs). Zero-value coefficient estimates occur when there is insufficient variation in the explanatory variable.

Source: Authors' calculations.

to trade with OECD member countries (thus excluding South-South trade in services).

The model incorporates indicator variables for over 500 FTAs, grouped into nine prominent individual FTAs and groups of FTAs worldwide, including the North American Free Trade Agreement (NAFTA) and FTAs undertaken by the European Union. The FTA indicators are dichotomous (0, 1) variables, often termed dummy variables. They take a value of 1 if partner countries are FTA members and their mutual trade agreement is in force; they take a value of 0 otherwise.

In the gravity model, each observation of bilateral trade, denoted by T_{ij}, is indexed by exporting country i and importing country j. Given that import data reported by national authorities are generally more reliable than export data, the bilateral trade flows (T_{ij}) are compiled in the main dataset using import data by reporting countries with all recorded partners. Where observations are missing, however, export data by reporting countries are used to fill out the dataset.

For both merchandise and services trade, the new gravity model dataset includes observations not only for aggregate bilateral trade but also for trade disaggregated by "1-digit" SITC categories.[6] And for all observations, the value of trade reported in US dollars is converted to real terms in each year using the US consumer price index for all urban consumers.[7] With regard to the merchandise trade data, special care is taken with the organization of the data for certain countries: (1) Taiwan trade is assumed equal to trade by "Other Asia, nes" in the Comtrade database (Taiwan is omitted from the database because of its political exclusion from the United Nations); (2) Belgium and Luxembourg are treated as a single country, Belgium-Luxembourg, until the 1990s; (3) Germany is integrated under a single country code, though the trade of Germany before the early 1990s in the Comtrade database is separately identified as trade by the Federal Republic of Germany; and (4) Russia and the newly independent states of Eastern Europe are not included in the trade dataset until the year of their independence, and no consideration is given to the trade of these states before the collapse of the Soviet Union and the end of Soviet hegemony over Eastern Europe.

In this application, bilateral trade values less than $10 million were dropped in order to estimate coefficients that are appropriate for significant trade flows. When small trade flows are included, the logarithmic specification of the gravity model gives equal weight, in estimating coefficients, to a bilateral trade increase from $1 million to $2 million and an increase from $100 million to $200 million. Since the matrix of world trade includes numerous small flows between small and distant countries, those flows will dominate the coefficient estimates unless they are dropped. However, dropping the small flows leads to an anomalous negative estimate for the coefficient on the Generalized System of Preferences (GSP).[8] In any event, it seems unlikely that Cuba would be eligible for GSP from the United States, even with complete normalization, because US imports of most Cuban products would substantially exceed the "competitive need" test established in the US GSP statute.[9]

---

6. For the categories, see http://unstats.un.org/unsd/cr/registry/regcst.asp?Cl=8&Lg=1.

7. The use of the consumer price index (CPI) to deflate prices follows Rose (2004). For merchandise trade, the producer price index (PPI) seems more appropriate. However, the correlation between monthly levels of the CPI and PPI between 2000 and 2008 is nearly perfect, with an R-squared value of 0.97. In any event, the CPI seems more appropriate for services trade.

8. Table 6.1 reports a negative GSP coefficient, –0.268, for merchandise trade. Dropping bilateral trade flows under $10 million excludes a great many exports from small GSP countries. When these are included, the GSP coefficient is positive and significant, 0.186.

9. Competitive need limits (CNLs) set quantitative limits for GSP benefits. Products eligible for the GSP are classified by the US Customs and Border Protection by 8-digit tariff lines of the Harmonized Tariff Schedule of the United States (HTSUS). For a beneficiary developing country (BDC) to continue to receive benefits, US imports of a BDC product cannot exceed (1) 50 percent or more of total US imports of that product or (2) a specific dollar value threshold, e.g., set at $160 million in 2013 and raised to $165 million in 2014. If imports from a BDC exceed one of these

The explanatory variables included in the new gravity model dataset are drawn from three primary sources. First, the observations on such "standard" time-invariant variables as distance between trading partners and countries' shared geographical and national characteristics (common border, language, colonial relationships, etc.) are drawn from a prominent gravity model dataset developed by Rose (2004).[10] Second, observations on nine major individual and groups of preferential trading arrangements are drawn from the previous gravity model datasets (using proprietary information) with updates to the indicator for the European Union to reflect the EU enlargement since 2005. Finally, World Bank and UN Conference on Trade and Development (UNCTAD) data are used to specify real GDP and GDP per capita series for all countries.

Trade Potential

Table 6.1 sets out the gravity model's estimation results for bilateral merchandise and services trade. The R-squared value for this model indicates that the specified explanatory variables contribute to explaining 65 percent of the logarithmic variation in bilateral trade flows. In terms of the specified explanatory variables displayed in table 6.1, as expected, increased distance between partners would reduce both merchandise and services trade, with a larger impact on merchandise trade. A greater joint GDP increases bilateral trade, all other variables held constant. A common language and land border both increase bilateral trade, as does the fact of one (or both) of the partners being an island. A strong message from table 6.1 is the supercharged trade effect of several FTAs, particularly NAFTA. The estimated coefficient on NAFTA for merchandise trade is 1.372, which, when applied as an exponent to the natural number e, suggests an increase of almost 300 percent through a "NAFTA effect"—too large to seem believable. The merchandise trade coefficient for "Other FTAs" (reflecting agreements such as the Central American Free Trade Agreement–Dominican Republic) is 0.630, which suggests an 88 percent increase in merchandise trade flows from a free trade agreement. This coefficient seems far more plausible and is the one we use to forecast the merchandise trade outcome of a possible free trade agreement between the United States and Cuba (this possibility is explored in chapter 7). The estimated services coefficient for NAFTA seems reasonable at 0.312, implying a trade increase of 37 percent.

In table 6.2, we apply the estimated coefficients from table 6.1 to predict potential bilateral trade between the United States and Cuba in the wake of economic normalization—not a free trade agreement, just normalization. Actual trade between the two countries is quite modest, with no recorded

---

limits, they are considered "sufficiently competitive" and GSP treatment is thereby suspended unless the country meets the criteria for a CNL waiver; see Jones (2013).

10. One of the explanatory variables in the Rose (2004) dataset, "common country" has no statistical effect in the present analysis (table 6.1). This variable identifies separate countries that were once a single country, such as Pakistan and Bangladesh or the Czech Republic and Slovakia.

Table 6.2   Actual versus potential US-Cuba merchandise trade based on gravity model estimates, 2005–11

| | US-Cuba merchandise trade (actuals and with normalization) | | | | | | US-Cuba merchandise trade (with US-Cuba FTA) | |
| | Actual trade (millions of US dollars) | | Potential trade (millions of US dollars) | | Trade shortfall (percent) | | Potential trade (millions of US dollars) | |
Year	US exports to Cuba	Cuban exports to United States	US exports to Cuba	Cuban exports to United States	US exports to Cuba	Cuban exports to United States	US exports to Cuba	Cuban exports to United States
2005	361	0	2,982	3,972	87.9	100.0	5,599	7,459
2006	348	0	3,398	4,527	89.8	100.0	6,381	8,500
2007	447	0	3,722	4,958	88.0	100.0	6,988	9,310
2008	718	0	3,918	5,219	81.7	100.0	7,356	9,799
2009	533	0	3,924	5,228	86.4	100.0	7,368	9,816
2010	370	0	4,117	5,485	91.0	100.0	7,730	10,298
2011	352	0	4,322	5,757	91.9	100.0	8,114	10,809

FTA = free trade agreement

Notes: Potential trade levels are based on the gravity model estimates for real trade for 2000–08 in table 6.1, adjusted to nominal values using the US consumer price index (the gravity model trade value deflator) and recent observations for the model's explanatory variables. The predicted levels of US-Cuba trade are adjusted to conform to ratios of imports to exports for US trade with Mexico in 2011. Trade shortfalls are computed as 100*[(potential – actual)/potential]. Predicted merchandise trade with an FTA between the United States and Cuba is based on the "Other FTAs" coefficient in table 6.1, namely 0.630, implying a multiple of 1.8776 times the predicted trade values without an FTA.

Source: Actual merchandise trade levels, customs values for US imports, and free on board values for US exports, respectively, from and to Cuba, are compiled from US International Trade Commission (USITC) Trade DataWeb, http://dataweb.usitc.gov. Potential trade levels based on authors' calculations.

Cuban exports to the United States and US exports to Cuba limited to specific agricultural and humanitarian items. The model indicates very significant merchandise trade shortfalls in both directions—in 2011, around 90 percent shortfall for US exports to Cuba and 100 percent shortfall for Cuban exports to the United States. With normalization, the gravity model suggests that US merchandise exports to Cuba might reach $4.3 billion annually, comparable to US exports to the Dominican Republic ($7.3 billion in 2011) or El Salvador ($3.4 billion in 2011). Cuban merchandise exports to the United States might reach $5.8 billion annually, somewhat greater than exports from the Dominican Republic ($3.3 billion) or El Salvador ($2.4 billion).

These estimates suggest that, with normalization, the United States would experience a bilateral merchandise trade deficit with Cuba of about $1.5 billion annually. Observers who view trade relations through a mercantilistic lens ("exports good, imports bad") will find this prospect disagreeable for the United States but agreeable for Cuba. We think the mercantilistic lens is badly flawed, because both exports and imports deliver benefits to each trading partner through multiple channels—lower consumer costs, higher firm productivity, greater variety, and better allocation of resources. In any event, the projected bilateral merchandise trade deficit with Cuba is small in the overall scheme of US external commerce with the world (two-way merchandise trade flows of around $3.8 trillion annually) and might be partly offset by a US surplus in services trade with Cuba (discussed below).

More than a decade ago, the US International Trade Commission (USITC 2001) tried to estimate potential US merchandise exports to Cuba based on average 1996-98 Cuban trade with the world.[11] In that period, Cuban merchandise imports from the world totaled $3.8 billion. The USITC estimated that, in the absence of US sanctions, US exports would account for 17 to 27 percent of Cuban imports, totaling somewhere between $658 million and $1,047 million. This range is considerably below our estimate of $4.3 billion. One reason is that Cuban merchandise imports from the world in 2011 were $8.8 billion versus the $3.8 billion average for 1996-98. That factor alone would more than double a current estimate following the USITC methodology. Equally important, however, is that an elimination of sanctions would sharply boost Cuban exports to the United States (table 6.2), which in turn—through the mechanism of larger Cuban income—would attract far more US exports to Cuba. Our gravity model methodology does a better job of capturing these forces than the earlier USITC methodology.

The impact is similar in direction, although less dramatic, for trade in services. Currently there is no recorded services trade between the United States and Cuba.[12] US services exporters, according to table 6.3, are missing

---

11. The USITC (2001) report was summarized by Coleman (2001).

12. Although there is no officially recorded bilateral trade in services, data can be found on the number of Cuban-Americans and Americans who travel to Cuba each year, estimated to be between 300,000 and 400,000 annually (Sullivan 2012a).

Table 6.3 Actual versus potential US-Cuba services trade based on gravity model estimates, 2005–11

| | US-Cuba trade in services (actuals and with normalization) | | | | | | US-Cuba services trade (with US-Cuba FTA) | |
| | Actual trade (millions of US dollars) | | Potential trade (millions of US dollars) | | Trade shortfall (percent) | | Potential trade (millions of US dollars) | |
Year	US exports to Cuba	Cuban exports to United States	US exports to Cuba	Cuban exports to United States	US exports to Cuba	Cuban exports to United States	US exports to Cuba	Cuban exports to United States
2005	0	0	1,054	608	100.0	100.0	1,440	831
2006	0	0	1,219	703	100.0	100.0	1,666	961
2007	0	0	1,347	777	100.0	100.0	1,840	1,061
2008	0	0	1,422	820	100.0	100.0	1,942	1,120
2009	0	0	1,418	818	100.0	100.0	1,938	1,118
2010	0	0	1,495	862	100.0	100.0	2,042	1,178
2011	0	0	1,574	908	100.0	100.0	2,151	1,240

FTA = free trade agreement

Notes: Potential trade levels are based on the gravity model estimates for real trade in services for 2000–08 in table 6.1, adjusted to nominal values using the US consumer price index (the gravity model trade value deflator) and recent observations for the model's explanatory variables. The predicted levels of US-Cuba trade are adjusted to conform to the ratio of imports to exports for US trade with Mexico in 2010. Trade shortfalls are computed as 100*(potential − actual)/potential]. Services trade with an FTA between the United States and Cuba is based on the NAFTA coefficient in table 6.1, namely 0.312, implying a multiple of 1.3662 times the predicted trade without an FTA.

Source: Potential trade levels based on authors' calculations.

out on potential sales of $1.6 billion to Cuba, and Cuban services exporters are missing out on potential sales of $0.9 billion to the United States.

Investment Potential

Data limitations preclude the use of a gravity model for predicting US and world FDI in Cuba in the wake of economic normalization. Instead we draw on simple comparisons with other countries in the region (table 6.4). As the data show, currently the world FDI stock in Cuba is trivial, under $500 million, and the US stock is virtually zero. With normalization, we think Cuba could soon attract at least as much FDI stock as the Dominican Republic, $17 billion from the world and nearly $2 billion from the United States. Possibly Cuba could attract much more because of its tourist, medical, beverage, and agricultural potential.

But Jamaica's experience in recent years sounds a cautionary note, at least for investment from the United States. Jamaica is afflicted with the three Cs: cocaine, crime, and corruption, and these woes drive foreign investors away.[13] World FDI in Jamaica has stalled at around $11 billion, and US FDI stock has dropped sharply, from around $3 billion in the early 1990s to under $600 million in 2011. If Cuba post-Castro is engulfed by the three Cs, the country is not likely to attract much FDI from the United States, whatever the extent of political and economic normalization.

---

13. While corruption seriously afflicts some Asian countries that attract large amounts of FDI (including China), the work of Beata S. Javorcik and Shang-Jin Wei (2009), among others, establishes that corruption is, by and large, a negative factor. Moreover, crime and cocaine are effectively controlled across most of Asia.

Table 6.4   Foreign direct investment (FDI) stock in selected countries, 2000–11 (millions of US dollars)

Country	2000	2001	2002	2003	2004	2005	2006	2007	2008	2009	2010	2011
World outward FDI to												
Cuba	74	78	81	74	77	93	119	182	207	231	317	427
Dominican Republic	1,673	2,752	3,669	3,598	3,956	5,276	6,375	8,082	10,961	13,106	14,731	17,103
Guatemala	3,420	3,918	4,124	4,387	4,683	3,319	3,898	4,618	5,439	5,636	6,518	7,709
Jamaica	3,317	3,931	4,410	5,130	5,732	6,919	7,801	8,667	10,104	10,628	10,855	11,097
US outward FDI to												
Cuba	(D)	(D)	−25	−26	(D)	−2	−2	−2	−2	−2	−2	−2
Dominican Republic	1,143	1,116	983	816	1,028	815	789	712	806	1,065	1,289	1,710
Guatemala	835	311	300	298	410	386	436	614	1,188	971	1,064	1,100
Jamaica	2,483	2,957	3,097	3,406	3,551	1,018	940	801	940	708	570	567

Note: (D) indicates that data in the cell have been suppressed to avoid disclosure of data of individual companies.

Source: US Bureau of Economic Analysis, 2012, www.bea.gov/international; UNCTADStat database, 2012, http://unctadstat.unctad.org.

7

Brass Tacks: Deeper Integration

Following the path taken by Mexico, Central America, and several Caribbean countries, Cuba would benefit enormously from deeper integration with the US economy. Past experience proves that deep integration substantially augments the cross-border flows of goods, services, and investment. More important, deep integration raises living standards, especially in the smaller partner country. But the path to deep integration is not easy: Partner countries must take politically difficult steps to embrace the tenets of a market economy, covering everything from trade barriers to investment to labor rights. In this chapter we describe several markers on the path to deep integration. The subjects we have chosen are not exhaustive but they do illustrate the challenges if Cuba decides that it wants more than an arm's-length commercial relation with the United States.

Investment Agreements

At least 90 percent of the heavy lifting to make Cuba an attractive location for investment needs to be done in Havana. The recorded stock of inward foreign direct investment (FDI) in Cuba is less than $500 million (population 11.2 million),[1] compared with $17 billion in the Dominican Republic (population 10.2 million) or $16 billion in Costa Rica (population 4.8 million) (UNCTAD 2012). In his informative report, Richard Feinberg (2012) reports multiple

---

1. Feinberg (2012) puts the FDI stock at $3.5 billion, based on cumulated inflows to 2009. Even if correct, this figure is well below FDI stocks in comparable countries, measured on a per capita basis or relative to GDP.

differences between the enticing investment climate in Costa Rica and the daunting climate in Cuba. Obvious differences run the gamut from property rights to labor practices to physical infrastructure. If Cuba wants serious FDI, the country will need to upgrade its practices.

That said, Cuba made a small start in 1982 when it passed Decree-Law 50, which allowed foreign investment in principle but with so many restrictions that very little FDI arrived. In 1992, Cuba amended its Constitution, giving somewhat more scope to foreign investors. A bigger change came in the mid-1990s when Cuba passed the Foreign Investment Act (Law 77) in 1995 and then issued Decree-Law 165 in 1996, permitting free zones and industrial parks. But the take-up was modest. Approvals are slow for several reasons: Multinational corporations are generally required to form joint ventures with state enterprises (tourism and mining are exceptions), they must employ Cubans vetted by the government, and they are subject to price controls and other interference from government officials (see box 7.1).

Cuba could make a fresh start at improving its investment climate by accepting, on a phased timetable, the suite of investment agreements typically offered by the United States.

Joint Commission on Trade and Investment

The gentle starting point for a US-Cuba investment agreement could be a Joint Commission on Trade and Investment (JCTI). This is basically a "get-acquainted" dialogue between policy officials. For example, in the US-Uruguay JCTI (established in 2002 as a bilateral mechanism to strengthen coordination on common trade and investment objectives), the parties discussed six areas: customs issues, intellectual property protection, investment, labor, environment, and trade in goods.[2] Among these areas, the greatest attention was paid to investment, particularly policies that either discourage or prohibit inward FDI. The JCTI talks served as a launching pad for the eventual US-Uruguay Bilateral Investment Treaty, which entered into force on November 1, 2006.[3]

---

2. US State Department, "U.S. Relations with Uruguay," fact sheet, November 2012, www.state.gov/r/pa/ei/bgn/2091.htm (accessed on March 14, 2013). For details on the JCTI, see "US-Uruguay Joint Declaration of Signing of Agreement Establishing a Joint Commission on Trade and Investment," US Embassy Montevideo, April 11, 2002, http://archives.uruguay.usembassy.gov (accessed on March 20, 2013).

3. See USTR, "U.S., Uruguay Hold Trade and Investment Council Meeting," press release, June 2009, www.ustr.gov/about-us/press-office/press-releases/2009/june/us-uruguay-hold-trade-and-investment-council-meeting (accessed on March 20, 2013).

Box 7.1 History of Cuban laws governing foreign direct investment (FDI)

1982: First law on FDI

Decree-Law 50 (or "Law 50") was designed to attract foreign capital by allowing joint ventures. But it set a ceiling of 49 percent foreign ownership, ensuring that Cuban state-owned enterprises maintained a controlling share. The restrictive nature of the law resulted in very little FDI; the first FDI project was not completed until 1990.

1992: Amendment to the Cuban Constitution

Following the collapse of the Soviet Union, the Cuban government enacted reforms to promote FDI. The Constitution was amended to allow property ownership and/or transfer state property to joint ventures with foreign capital. Amendments to the Constitution also exempted joint ventures from taxes on gross income, personal income, and the transfer of real estate and business property; eliminated customs duties for certain "necessary" equipment; allowed the repatriation in hard currency of some earnings (e.g., salaries of foreign employees); removed restrictions on hiring foreign executive and technical personnel; and allowed 51 percent foreign ownership in special cases (e.g., in the tourism and mining sectors and where the foreign investor was Latin American).

1995: The Foreign Investment Act

The Foreign Investment Act, or Law 77, authorizes FDI in all sectors of the Cuban economy except defense, health care, and education. Under Law 77 three types of FDI are permitted: (1) joint ventures, (2) international economic association contracts (EAC), and (3) wholly foreign capital companies (investments may be 100 percent foreign capital). Law 77 also allows the creation of duty-free zones and industrial parks open to foreign investors. Law 77 prohibits expropriation of foreign investments, except for specific cases in the public interest, in which case compensation is required.

1996: Law 165

Law 165 established free trade zones. Foreign companies operating within the free trade zones do not pay profit or payroll taxes for 12 years and are 50 percent tax exempt for another five years. Companies can send 25 percent of their products to the domestic market duty-free and products with a 50 percent or more domestic value added can enter the domestic market duty-free.

Tax structure

Foreign investors that are party to a joint venture or EAC are exempt from personal income tax on dividends received from business profits. The capital gains tax is 30 percent for joint ventures and EACs, 35 percent for wholly foreign capital companies. No withholding tax is applied to dividends or interest paid to a foreign party in a joint venture or EAC. The payroll tax is 11 percent for joint ventures and EACs and 25 percent for wholly foreign capital companies.

Trade and Investment Framework Agreement

The most common US launching pad for either a free trade agreement (FTA) or bilateral investment treaty (BIT) is the trade and investment framework agreement (TIFA). According to the Congressional Research Service (CRS), TIFAs are formed "to consult on issues of mutual interest in order to facilitate trade and investment. TIFAs are non-binding, do not involve changes to US law, and therefore, do not require congressional approval. TIFAs may lead to free trade agreement negotiations" (Akhtar, Bolle, and Nelson 2013, 17).[4] The CRS could have added that a TIFA can also lead to a BIT, either as a chapter within an FTA or as a standalone agreement.

The United States has two TIFAs with countries in the Americas: the US–Caribbean Community (Caricom) TIFA (1991) and the US-Uruguay TIFA (2007).[5] The full list appears in box 7.2. The TIFA with Uruguay illustrates the timeline and achievements.[6] As it happened, the US-Uruguay BIT actually preceded the TIFA, so in this case the TIFA pointed more to the possibility of an FTA than a new investment agreement (though a bilateral FTA is not yet being negotiated). The TIFA also includes an annex that establishes a work program for addressing issues including intellectual property rights, regulatory issues, information and communications technology and electronic commerce, trade and technical capacity building, trade in services, and government procurement. The annex permits the TIFA council to add other issues to the program.

Bilateral Investment Treaty

Put simply, BITs "establish binding rules for the reciprocal protection of investment in each other's territories" (Akhtar, Bolle, and Nelson 2013). The United States currently has 41 BITs, most of which are with developing countries. Since they are treaties, US BITs must be ratified by the Senate, and ratification requires a two-thirds affirmative vote (67 affirmative, if all senators are present and voting).

---

4. Note that the names of TIFAs may vary—e.g., the Trade, Investment, and Development Cooperative Agreement (TIDCA) with the Southern African Customs Union. For details on the status of various US TIFAs, see USTR (2012).

5. The United States has signaled intent to complete negotiations in the near term on a revised "21st century TIFA" with Caricom.

6. On January 25, 2007, the United States and Uruguay signed the TIFA, which established a Trade and Investment Council (TIC). TIFA councils usually meet at least once a year at senior levels of government. On October 2, 2008, both sides signed protocols to the TIFA covering commitments in the areas of trade facilitation and trade and the environment.

Box 7.2 US trade and investment framework agreements (TIFAs), by region

Africa	Americas	Europe and the Middle East	Southeast Asia and the Pacific	South and Central Asia
US-Angola TIFA	US-Caribbean Community (Caricom) TIFA	US-Algeria TIFA	US-Association of Southeast Asian Nations (ASEAN) TIFA	US-Afghanistan TIFA
US-Common Market for Eastern and Southern Africa (COMESA) TIFA	US-Uruguay TIFA	US-Bahrain TIFA	US-Brunei TIFA	US-Central Asia TIFA
US-East African Community (EAC) TIFA		US-Egypt TIFA	US-Cambodia TIFA	US-Maldives TIFA
US-Ghana TIFA		US-Cooperation Council for the Arab States of the Gulf (GCC) Framework Agreement for Trade, Economic, Investment, and Technical Cooperation	US-Indonesia TIFA	US-Nepal TIFA
US-Mauritius TIFA		US-Iceland TICF	US-New Zealand TIFA	US-Pakistan TIFA
US-Mozambique TIFA		US-Iraq TIFA	US-Philippines TIFA	US-Sri Lanka TIFA
US-Nigeria TIFA		US-Kuwait TIFA	US-Thailand TIFA	
US-Rwanda TIFA		US-Lebanon TIFA	US-Vietnam TIFA	
US-South Africa TIFA		US-Libya TIFA		
US-Southern African Customs Union (SACU) Trade, Investment, and Development Cooperative Agreement		US-Oman TIFA		
US-West African Economic and Monetary Union (WAEMU) TIFA		US-Qatar TIFA		
		US-Saudi Arabia TIFA		
		US-Switzerland TICF		
		US-Tunisia TIFA		
		US-Turkey TIFA		
		US-Ukraine TICA		
		US-United Arab Emirates (UAE) TIFA		
		US-Yemen TIFA		

TICF = trade and investment cooperation forum; TICA = trade and investment cooperation agreement

According to the US Trade Representative, US BITs provide US investors with six core benefits:[7]

1. Investors and "covered investments" are afforded both national treatment (i.e., "treated as favorably as the host party treats its own investors and their investments") and most favored nation treatment (i.e., "treated as favorably as investors and investments from any third country") for all phases of investment.[8]

2. Limits are established on expropriation and "prompt, adequate, and effective compensation" is required when expropriation occurs.

3. Ability to transfer investment-related funds across borders is ensured "without delay and using a market rate of exchange."

4. Restrictions are set forth on performance requirements, such as local content requirements.

5. The right to employ top managerial personnel, regardless of nationality, is guaranteed.

6. The right to international arbitration for an investment dispute with the host country government is ensured, with no requirement to use domestic courts.

The BIT has historical antecedents (such as the Friendship, Commerce, and Navigation treaties negotiated by the United States between 1778 and 1967), but the first recognized BIT was signed between Germany and Pakistan in 1959. BITs took off slowly, but today the number exceeds 2,800 (UNCTAD 2012).

Like other developing countries, Cuba has entered into numerous BITs. The first Cuban BIT was with Italy, signed in 1993. By 2013, Cuba had signed 61 BITs (though 20 of them remain to be ratified by both parties). While Spain has a BIT with Cuba, Canada, another major investor, does not. The Cuban treaties contain several standard provisions:[9]

- They include language fostering cooperation and encouraging foreign investment.

- They contain a broad definition of investment, including not only bricks and mortar but also intellectual property rights, certain financial assets, and government concessions.

- Returns on investment are entitled to equivalent protection as the original investment.

---

7. Core benefits of US BITs are drawn from USTR, "Bilateral Investment Treaties," www.ustr.gov.

8. Phases of investment cover the "full life-cycle of investment," including establishment or acquisition, management, operation, expansion, and disposition.

9. This section draws heavily on Pérez-López and Travieso-Diaz (2001).

- With extensive exceptions, the BITs provide for rights of establishment, national treatment, and most favored nation treatment.

- The BITs promise "prompt, adequate and effective" compensation (or words of similar effect) in the event of expropriation.

- In the event of investment disputes, BITs generally provide for arbitration of state-to-state and investor-state disputes.

A functioning arbitration system for resolving bilateral investment disputes is an important feature for expanding FDI in Cuba. In the past decade, the use of arbitration has increased through Cuba's Arbitration Court of Foreign Trade (ACFT) and the Cuban Court of International Commercial Arbitration (CCICA), which replaced the ACFT in 2007. The ACFT resolved 181 cases from 1965 to 1990 and 478 cases from 1990 to 2006, with more than half processed during the 2000s.[10] Kevin Tuininga (2008) suggests that the recent increase in submitted disputes could be evidence of the "heightened confidence in the impartiality and effectiveness of arbitration proceedings in Cuba."

Given Cuba's enthusiasm for BITs, an agreement with the United States might seem an easy proposition. But BITs come in different flavors, and the current US model BIT may be the most demanding in contemporary usage. The US model was updated in 2012 after three years of interagency review and calls for tougher standards than the already demanding 2004 model.[11] In fact, the 2004 US model has, so far, been accepted only by Uruguay and Rwanda, and negotiations with India, Pakistan, and China, using the 2012 US model, are moving slowly. From the standpoint of aspiring partners, the more difficult features of the latest US model include

- strong transparency obligations on matters affecting investment, applied not only to government agencies but also to state-owned enterprises;

- advance publication of proposed laws and regulations and an opportunity to comment;

- commitment not to require the use of technologies that give a preference to domestic companies and commitment to allow foreign firms a voice in setting technical standards; and

- commitments not to waive or derogate from the operation of domestic laws that protect labor or the environment, coupled with commitments to enforce domestic laws in these areas and to recognize International Labor Organization (ILO) declarations and multilateral environmental agree-

---

10. In the early 2000s, the majority of cases involved Spain, Panama, and Italy. The decisions for one notable case—a state-to-state dispute between Italy and Cuba in 2003—were recently published: An ad hoc tribunal ruled in Cuba's favor in 2008, rejecting Italy's claims either on jurisdictional grounds or on merits. For details, see Potestà (2012).

11. For more details on the 2012 revisions to the US model BIT, see USTR, "Fact Sheet on Model Bilateral Investment Treaty," April 2012, www.ustr.gov; and Johnson (2012).

ments (such as the Montreal Protocol or the Convention on International Trade in Endangered Species).

Specifically, the 2012 US model amends "nonderogable" labor rights to include all four core labor rights under the ILO 1998 Declaration,[12] in addition to the right to acceptable conditions of work (Prislan and Zandvliet 2013).[13] Expanded labor obligations in the BIT framework could be a challenge for Cuba, which, despite being a signatory of 89 ILO conventions, has a long-standing history of violations, including the Freedom of Association and Protection of the Right to Organize (Convention 87), Protection of Wages (Convention 95), and the Right to Organize and Collective Bargaining (Convention 98) (see Perales 2010).

Reciprocity Measures

Once bilateral political relations are normalized, the United States and Cuba will be eager to promote investment. US firms will profit handsomely from investment opportunities, while Cuba will benefit greatly from increased access to foreign capital, technology, and services. To facilitate this process, the United States and Cuba should enter into a TIFA and start consultation on issues of mutual interest. The nonbinding properties of a TIFA and its open-ended nature outlined in the previous section make a TIFA an ideal stepping stone toward deeper bilateral investment ties, possibly in the form of a BIT.

In exchange for access to large volumes of capital and expertise, Cuba should implement reforms to ensure US firms are treated the same as both Cuban enterprises and established foreign investors like Canada and Spain. That means US investors should be given the right to participate in joint ventures and economic association contracts and establish wholly owned companies. Likewise, the United States should allow Cuban firms to invest in the United States. Additionally, the United States should press Cuba to reform its labor practices such as the system of wage determination, decisions to hire and fire, and collective action rights and responsibilities, which are generally considered to be inconsistent with ILO standards.

---

12. The core labor rights as established by the ILO Declaration on Fundamental Principles and Rights of Work include (1) freedom of association and the effective recognition of the right to collective bargaining, (2) elimination of all forms of forced or compulsory labor, (3) effective abolition of child labor, and (4) elimination of discrimination in respect of employment and occupation.

13. However, Prislan and Zandvliet (2013) also note that while the commitments to labor standards are more demanding in the 2012 US model, the BIT still "lacks clear obligation to adopt and maintain ILO standards as a minimum, and does not allow disputes to be submitted to arbitration."

Intellectual Property Rights

As outlined in chapter 3, Cuba participates in a number of important multilateral agreements related to intellectual property rights (IPRs), including 16 World Intellectual Property Organization (WIPO) treaties, as well as the World Trade Organization (WTO) Agreement on Trade-Related Aspects of Intellectual Property Rights (TRIPS), which establishes minimum standards for the protection and enforcement of IPRs.[14] Intellectual property provisions in Cuba's bilateral and regional agreements are generally more limited in scope. Most of Cuba's BITs include coverage of intellectual property, but these provisions vary in standards of protection, definitions of IPRs, and recourse to dispute settlement procedures.

As a developing country, Cuba has faced challenges bringing its laws and judicial processes up to speed with international standards and needs to improve its IPR enforcement mechanisms. However, Cuba has instituted a series of legislative changes that aim to align its domestic IPR regime with commitments under the TRIPS Agreement. In part, this was motivated by Cuba's desire to attract FDI and expand the global reach of its pharmaceutical and biotechnology sectors (see Reid-Henry 2010). Cuba has gained international recognition in the development of meningitis and hepatitis vaccines and cancer therapy drugs. Scientific skill combined with the quality of Cuba's intellectual property in the biotech field has been lauded as a success story for attracting joint ventures with foreign partners including Canadian, Indian, and Malaysian firms (WIPO 2004). Given its interest in these sectors, Cuba participates actively in the ongoing global dialogue on the standards of patent protection.[15]

Strengthening intellectual property protection is intended not only to stimulate innovation in key sectors but also to create a business environment that attracts international commercial transactions.[16] While the number of

---

14. Specifically, TRIPS provisions cover copyrights, trademarks including geographical indications, patents, industrial designs, integrated circuit designs, and protection of undisclosed information (e.g., trade secrets and know-how). In addition to standards of protection, TRIPS establishes enforcement measures including civil and administrative procedures and remedies, border measures, and criminal procedures. For a detailed summary, see Ilias and Fergusson (2011).

15. In the early 2000s, Cuba was among a group of developing countries concerned about facilitating access to generic drugs for poor countries with insufficient manufacturing capacities in the pharmaceutical sector and sought to enlarge the scope of compulsory licensing as a tool provided under TRIPS for this purpose. In the recent debate over the patentability of plant and animal inventions, Cuba, along with India, Brazil, Bolivia, and other developing countries, has been pushing for an amendment to the TRIPS Agreement that would require patent applicants to disclose the origin of genetic resources and any traditional knowledge used in the inventions.

16. It is widely acknowledged that reforming IPRs in itself is not enough to promote economic growth and development, rather the "IPR regime must be embedded in an overall development strategy, including investments in education and human capital, improvements in public health, and support for domestic innovation and adoption technology" (Maskus 2012).

Table 7.1 Intellectual property filings in Cuba and by Cubans abroad, 1997–2012

Type of filing	Filed or granted in Cuba			Filed or granted abroad
	Resident	Nonresident	Total	
Patents				
Applications	682	1,256	1,938	1,310
Patents granted	360	455	815	582
Trademarks				
Applications	4,697	34,274	38,971	4,378
Registrations	3,937	30,781	34,718	3,696
Industrial designs				
Applications	381	105	486	286
Registrations	293	116	409	288

Notes: Resident filing refers to an application filed in Cuba by its own resident; nonresident filing refers to an application filed by a foreigner in Cuba; an abroad filing refers to an application filed by a Cuban resident in a foreign office. Cumulative totals represent the most complete data available, but data may be missing for some years or for the reporting office.

Source: World Intellectual Property Organization Statistical Database, Cuba Statistical Country Profile, updated December 2012, www.wipo.int/ipstats/en/statistics/country_profile/countries/cu.html.

intellectual property applications in Cuba is relatively small, foreign applications make up a significant share of total intellectual property filings in Cuba (see table 7.1). According to WIPO statistics, between 1997 and 2011, around 2,000 patent applications and about 39,000 trademark applications were filed in Cuba, with foreigners accounting for 65 and 88 percent, respectively. Globally, Cuban companies and nationals have submitted about 1,300 patent applications and 4,400 trademark applications abroad.[17] Nearly 44 percent of patent applications were in pharmaceuticals and 30 percent in biotechnology. These figures translate to nearly 600 patents granted and 3,700 trademark registrations obtained by Cubans abroad.[18]

Intellectual property rights have been a key issue for US and Cuban companies anticipating market access in the event economic relations are normalized. Companies and nationals from both countries are permitted to submit applications for patents, trademarks, and copyright protection through the US Patent and Trademark Office (USPTO) and US Copyright Office and Cuba's

17. The majority of Cuban intellectual property applications abroad are filed on a bilateral basis. Cuba has only minimally used the international processes established by WIPO-administered treaties, submitting a total of 300 patent and trademark applications via the Patent Cooperation Treaty and Madrid Protocol. These systems establish harmonized filing procedures by which an applicant may file a single patent application for multiple countries.

18. These figures are based on the available data through WIPO statistics, but due to missing data for certain years they likely underestimate the current total.

Industrial Property Office (OCPI). To date, Cuban companies have registered an estimated 100 patents and trademarks in the United States, and reportedly US companies have registered more than 5,000 trademarks in Cuba. However, in the race to secure distribution rights, a series of IPR disputes between the United States and Cuba have risen over brand name ownership and the use of trademarks of Cuban origin. Moreover, a US statute regarding the nonrecognition of rights in confiscated Cuban trademarks was found to be in violation of certain obligations under the WTO TRIPS Agreement. As Cuba continues to take steps to improve its domestic IPR regime, the United States and Cuba should address long-standing IPR disputes (discussed below).

Intellectual Property Laws in Cuba

Cuba has enacted a number of domestic laws on intellectual property protection. Over the years, a series of amendments have expanded the scope and coverage of IPRs. The basic provisions on copyright protection are established in Law 14, which was issued in 1977. In 1994, the law was amended to extend the period of copyright protection embedded in Articles 43, 45, and 47 of the 1977 law. Specifically, the term of protection for works, including joint works and works published anonymously, was extended from 25 to 50 years after the author's death or first publication of the work.[19] The term of protection for photographic works and visual arts was extended from 10 to 25 years.

Other core legislation includes Decree-Law 68 on Inventions, Scientific Discoveries, Industrial Designs, Trademarks, and Appellations of Origin, which was issued in 1983 and broadly regulates inventions. Under this law, the right to an invention could be granted through a certificate of patent or a certificate of author of invention, which is a *sui generis* form of protection recognizing the ownership of the author but granting the state exclusive rights to the use and commercialization of the invention (Sotolongo 2011). In this way, the development of intellectual property rights in Cuba saw "ownership...codified in terms of a more local, socialist rationality" (Reid-Henry 2010). A series of amendments to Decree-Law 68 broadened the scope of intellectual property protection: (1) in 1995, Decree-Law 160 expanded patent protection for pharmaceuticals and agricultural and chemical products; (2) in 1999, Decree-Law 203 expanded protections for trademarks and other distinctive signs[20] (e.g., figurative signs, sounds, colors, three-dimensional objects, etc.) and also in-

---

19. These periods of protection are generally comparable to those of other developing countries and meet the minimum standards set by TRIPS. In the case of the United States, the copyright protection term for all works including joint works is set at 70 years after the author's death; for anonymous and pseudonymous works, the term of protection is set at 95 years from the first publication or 120 years from the year of creation.

20. For trademarks and commercial slogans registration is binding and ensures exclusive rights, whereas for trade names, signs, and company emblems, registration is a "declaration of rights," which must be sealed by "first use in commerce"; otherwise competitors can file a cancellation action for nonuse (Sotolongo 2011).

cluded provisions on customs enforcement measures, including recourse to a temporary restraining order or seizure of goods (Sanchelima 2002); and (3) in 2002, Decree-Law 228 expanded trademark protections for geographical indications.[21]

In 2012, new laws went into effect, resulting in a number of changes that helped meet Cuba's obligations under TRIPS: Inventions, Industrial Designs, and Models (Decree-Law 290), the Protection of Plant Varieties (Decree-Law 291), and Layout Designs of Integrated Circuits (Decree-Law 292). To summarize, important changes include the following:[22]

■ Patents are permitted for genetically altered microorganisms. However, patents for inventions related to animals, plants, in addition to diagnostic, therapeutic, and surgical methods for treating humans or animals remain prohibited. These provisions comply with the exceptions under TRIPS.[23]

■ The term of patent protection was extended to 20 years. Previously, under Cuban law patents were only protected 10 years after the filing date with the possibility of an additional 5-year term extension.

■ Protection was afforded for utility models relating to small inventions, with a term of protection set at 10 years.

As the terms of intellectual property protection broadly improve in Cuba, strengthening enforcement mechanisms should also become a domestic priority. While Cuba maintains both civil and administrative procedures for processing claims, litigation in Cuba has generally not advanced beyond the trial level and many cases have been limited to appeals from administrative registration refusals (Sanchelima 2002). Moreover, Cuba has few laws on unfair competition and counterfeiting, and online piracy remains largely unregulated. Piracy of US goods including computer software and media content has become widespread in Cuba. Piracy is widely condoned by the Cuban government and attributed to pressures created by the US trade embargo.[24] Due to the absence of diplomatic relations, US companies have no official forum for addressing their complaints.

---

21. Cuba is among the WTO members that support the European Union's proposal to extend the higher level of geographical indication protection afforded to wines and spirits under the TRIPS Agreement to all foodstuffs and agricultural products.

22. Drawn from the summary of Lysaght & Co., "Cuba—New intellectual property laws," April 24, 2012, www.lysaght.co.uk/news_item.php?ID=135 (accessed on April 22, 2013).

23. See WTO, "Obligations and exceptions," fact sheet on TRIPS and pharmaceutical patents, September 2006, www.wto.org/english/tratop_e/trips_e/factsheet_pharm02_e.htm (accessed on December 19, 2013).

24. Esteban Israel, "Despite embargo, Cuba a haven for pirated U.S. goods," Reuters, September 2, 2010, www.reuters.com/article/2010/09/02/us-cuba-usa-piracy-idUSTRE6814IM20100902 (accessed on April 25, 2013).

US-Cuba Intellectual Property Disputes

To facilitate the exchange of intellectual property between the United States and Cuba, the Office of Foreign Assets Control (OFAC) included general licenses within the Cuban Assets Control Regulations (CACR), authorizing transactions by the Cuban government or any Cuban national relating to the registration and renewal of patents, trademarks, and copyrights with the USPTO or the US Copyright Office.[25] In addition, payments from Cuban nationals are authorized for fees due to the US government or due to attorneys or legal representation in connection with such activities. However, these general licenses were later amended to prohibit any transaction related to trademarks, trade names, or commercial names that are used in connection with assets confiscated by the Cuban government, unless the original owner or the owner's successor-in-interest expressly consented.[26]

Establishing trademark ownership and securing distribution rights are key IPR issues for both US and Cuban companies in anticipation of expanded access to their respective markets. But controversies have erupted in two contexts: (1) in the case of Cuban state-owned companies attempting to register trademarks in the United States that are the same or substantially similar to trademarks formerly used in connection with expropriated businesses and (2) in the case of non-Cuban companies registering brands in the United States that are claimed, by Cuba, to be strictly of Cuban origin. These were central issues in the high-profile disputes over the rights to Havana Club rum and Cohiba cigars.

Havana Club Rum Dispute

The most prominent IPR case has been the ongoing dispute over the Havana Club trademark between the Bermuda-based Bacardi & Co. and Havana Club Holding, S.A. (a joint venture between Cuba's state-owned company Cubaexport and the French company Pernod Ricard). The decades-long legal battle over rights to the use of the Havana Club trademark in the United States has prompted the United States to revise its legislation on the registration and protection of Cuban trademarks.[27]

The dispute over legal ownership of the trademark dates back to the 1960s.[28] The Cuban company José Arechabala (JASA) established the Havana Club brand for rum that was sold domestically in Cuba and also exported to

---

25. 31 CFR §515.527, "Certain transactions with respect to United States intellectual property."

26. This amendment was based on §211 of the Omnibus Appropriations Act, which the US Congress passed in 1998. This is discussed later in more detail.

27. For an extensive history of Bacardi rum and its relationship with Cuba and the Castro regime, see Gjelten (2009).

28. For more details on the origins and background of the dispute, see Kimmerling (1999).

the United States until 1960, when the company's assets were expropriated by the Cuban government. The state-owned company Cubaexport officially registered the trademark in the United States in 1976 and sought to transfer the rights to Havana Club Holding, when the joint venture was formed in 1993. However, OFAC revoked Havana Club Holding's transfer license under the US embargo, effectively invalidating the company's claim to the trademark in the United States (Kimmerling 1999). In 1995, the Arechabala family concluded an agreement with Bacardi & Co., whereby Bacardi purchased the "original" Havana Club trademark, the right to make and sell Havana Club rum, and remaining assets of the company.[29]

Bacardi sells limited quantities of rum in the United States (mostly in Florida) under the Havana Club trademark but labeled as manufactured in Puerto Rico. Upon marketing its own product in the United States, the Cuba-Pernod joint venture brought a case against Bacardi in the US federal courts, claiming that the use of the Havana Club trademark for non-Cuban rum misleads consumers as to the origin of Bacardi's rum.

In part a direct response to the ensuing legal battle, the US Congress passed the Omnibus Appropriations Act of 1990. Within the legislation, Section 211 ensured that (1) "unless the original owners have expressly consented, the US Patent and Trademark Office is prohibited from accepting or renewing the registration of a trademark, trade name, or commercial name by [another person]"; and (2) "US courts are prohibited from considering or enforcing the trademark claims of Cuban nationals (or their successors in interest) who acquired the trademark or trade name from the Cuban government...used in connection with property confiscated on or after January 1, 1959, without compensation to the original owners" (Lee 2004). The so-called Bacardi bill effectively prevented Cubaexport from transferring the US Havana Club registration to the Cuba-Pernod joint venture.

Amid concerns that such legislation violated the WTO TRIPS Agreement, the European Union initiated WTO dispute settlement procedures in 2000. After a series of proceedings, in 2002 the WTO Appellate Body ruled that the subsections of US law concerning court recognition and trademark enforcement were inconsistent with the national treatment and most favored nation nondiscrimination clauses of TRIPS. However, the decision also upheld the right of the United States to determine the criteria for trademark registration, including the right to "refuse the registration of confiscated marks."[30] The United States was asked to bring its measures into compliance with the WTO ruling by the beginning of 2003; however, Congress has yet to amend the Section 211 legislation.[31]

---

29. Whether the Arechabala family effectively allowed the original registration of the Havana Club trademark to "lapse" without applying for its renewal remains in contention.

30. For more details on the WTO rulings, see Lee (2004).

31. The deadline for the United States to comply with the final WTO rulings was extended multiple times due to stalled efforts to take legislative action amending Section 211. In 2005, the United

The US Congress has, however, explored two approaches to bringing Section 211 into compliance with the WTO TRIPS Agreement. Some legislators advocate a "narrow fix," which calls for an amendment that would apply Section 211 to US companies in addition to foreign companies, in order to affirm the principle that confiscated trademarks would not be recognized regardless of the nationality of the party claiming the rights (Sullivan 2012b). Others advocate repealing Section 211 as part of a broader bill that ends US sanctions against Cuba.[32] Those in favor of the broad approach are primarily concerned that a "narrow fix" might provoke Cuba to retaliate against the 500 US companies registered in Cuba that hold 5,000 existing trademarks.[33] To date, while Cuba continues to complain to the WTO Dispute Settlement Body about US failure to comply, there is no indication of retaliatory actions. Moreover, if Cuba wants to lay the groundwork for economic normalization, retaliation against existing trademark owners makes no sense.

Cubaexport's subsequent efforts to renew the Havana Club trademark have been unsuccessful. In 2006, OFAC declined the company's request for a license. Shortly after, the USPTO declared that the registration had expired. In 2011, the US Court of Appeals upheld the decision to deny Cubaexport's renewal of the trademark and, in May 2012, the US Supreme Court declined to review the case, officially sealing off the Cuban-Pernod joint venture from marketing the brand in the United States. Though the company continues to sell Havana Club rum in nearly 120 markets around the world, it has altered its strategy in the United States by preemptively registering a trademark for Havanista, a new brand of rum specifically aimed at the US market in the event economic relations are normalized.

Cohiba Cigars Dispute

Cohiba cigars were originally produced by the Cuban tobacco marketing company Cubatabaco and Habanos, S.A. during the 1960s as an exclusive product for the Cuban government and high-level officials. The cigars were first distrib-

---

States and the European Union signed a bilateral agreement whereby the European Union agreed it would not request authorization to retaliate, maintaining the right to do so at a later date. In effect, this agreement reduced pressure on the United States for timely compliance with the WTO.

32. Sullivan (2012b) summarizes the initiatives in the 112th Congress that reflect these two approaches. Specifically, two bills would apply the "narrow fix" (S 602 Nelson and HR 1166 Issa); while three broader bills seek to lift US sanctions on Cuba and also repeal Section 211 (HR 255 Serrano, HR 1887 Rangel, and HR 1888 Rangel).

33. Some observers have claimed that the US legislation also violates the Inter-American Convention for Trademark and Commercial Protection, to which both the United States and Cuba are parties, which could provide another basis for Cuban retaliation. In response to the US decision to block Cuba's registration of the Havana Club label, Maria de los Angeles Sanchez, director of the OCPI, stated, "the United States' disrespectful attitude in divesting the legitimate Cuban owners of the Havana Club brand can put at risk the brand and patent rights of American companies in our country."

uted commercially in the 1980s and Habanos formed a joint venture with the Spanish company Tabacalera, S.A. (later Altadis, S.A.) to distribute cigars internationally under the Cohiba brand. While the US embargo prevented distribution in the United States, by the early 2000s Cuba had registered the Cohiba name in nearly 120 markets.

However, in the late 1970s, the Cohiba trademark was registered in the United States by US-based Culbro Corporation and the trademark was subsequently renewed in 1992. The rights were licensed to General Cigar Company, which began distributing limited quantities of its cigars in the United States, labeled as manufactured in the Dominican Republic but "advertised as made from tobacco that is grown from Cuban seed" (Perry, Woods, and Shapiro 2000).

In 1997, Cubatabaco filed a claim with the USPTO seeking to invalidate Culbro's trademark based on the "famous marks doctrine," arguing that even in the absence of an official trademark registration, as a "well-known or famous name...[the Cohiba brand] should not be appropriated by a producer in another country" (Perry, Woods, and Shapiro 2000).[34] The ensuing lawsuit was based on claims of "trademark infringement, trade dress infringement, false designation of source or origin, unfair competition, misappropriation and trademark dilution" (Falk 1998). In 2004, the US federal court initially ruled in Cubatabaco's favor but, following a successful appeal by General Cigar, the original ruling was reversed. The final decision affirmed the validity of General Cigar's trademark registration and held that the US embargo precluded Cuba from obtaining property rights for an unregistered trademark.[35] In 2006, the US Supreme Court declined to review the case; however, Cuba has continued the litigation, most recently filing a motion for relief based on a claim of unfair competition by misappropriation.

Reciprocity Measures

Bilateral IPR issues are clearly intertwined in politics. However, we offer a few reciprocity suggestions to resolve the most acrimonious disputes. Once these "hot button" cases are settled, the United States and Cuba should find themselves in reasonable agreement on IPR questions.

---

34. The basis for this claim is established in Article 6bis of the Paris Convention for the Protection of Industrial Property, which states that "the countries of the Union undertake, ex officio if their legislation so permits, or at the request of an interested party, to refuse or to cancel the registration, and to prohibit the use, of a trademark which constitutes a reproduction, an imitation, or a translation, liable to create confusion, of a mark considered by the competent authority of the country of registration or use to be well known in that country as being already the mark of a person entitled to the benefits of this Convention and used for identical or similar goods." For the Paris Convention text, see www.wipo.int/treaties/en/ip/paris/trtdocs_wo020.html#P151_21198.

35. US courts continue to debate to what extent the famous marks doctrine is applicable to federal trademark infringement cases. For details, see Deinard and Stasik (2006).

Cuba should agree that Bacardi & Co. owns the Havana Club label for the US market provided that, within a reasonable period of time, Bacardi & Co. establishes a distilling plant in Cuba. Meanwhile, the United States should agree that Havana Club Holding, S.A. owns the Havana Club label for the rest of the world. The same division of the market should apply to the Cohiba label.

Next, as part of the normalization process, the United States should repeal Section 211, bringing the United States into compliance with the WTO TRIPS Agreement. To conclude the process, Cuba should establish a credible forum for resolving complaints related to IPR infringements, including those that relate to the piracy of copyrighted and patented goods, practices that are relatively widespread in Cuba.

Open Skies for Civilian Aircraft

The history of international civil aviation in the six decades since World War II is a record of slow liberalization. Civil aviation has gradually evolved from a complex network of bilateral air services agreements (ASAs), with selective "freedoms," to the current era of "open skies" in which countries allow carriers based in their partner countries all five operating "freedoms" (Hufbauer and Findlay 1996). Alongside this evolution, nearly all air fares and schedules are now deregulated: Carriers can charge what they wish, discriminate between types of passengers, change their fares on a moment's notice, schedule and discontinue flights, and alter departure and landing times. Weaker carriers have been acquired by stronger carriers in the wake of bankruptcy proceedings.

While all these changes have transformed global aviation, air travel between Cuba and the United States has also been liberalized, but to a lesser extent.[36] US charter operators offer direct flights to Cuba, but to do so they must hold a Carrier Service Providers (CSP) license from OFAC, which authorizes US commercial relations with Cuba, including the marketing of charter flights.[37] Moreover, individual passengers on charter flights must obtain a general or specific license from OFAC authorizing their travel to Cuba. Charter operators (e.g., Gulfstream Air Charter) can also supply all-cargo services between the United States and Cuba, but cargo "must be authorized under a License Exception set forth in the Export Administration Regulations or under a written export license issued by the US Department of Commerce."[38]

---

36. For a chronology of US policy toward Cuba travel restrictions, see Sullivan (2012a, 10).

37. While OFAC holds overall responsibility for administering economic and trade restrictions on Cuba, including travel and transportation, regulations published by the US Department of Transportation and US Department of Commerce also affect the operation of aircraft and the transportation of baggage/cargo. For an overview, see Lonnie Anne Pera, "U.S. Air Transportation Restrictions and Sanctions," Zukert, Scoutt & Rasenberger, LLP, January 31, 2013, www.zsrlaw.com/publications.

38. Silver Airways, "Cuba Charters," http://gulfstreamair.com/cuba.shtml.

Toward the end of the Clinton administration, at least seven charter operators with CSP licenses arranged weekly charter flights between three authorized US airports (Miami International Airport, John F. Kennedy International Airport, and Los Angeles International Airport) and five destinations in Cuba (Havana, Camagüey, Cienfuegos, Holguín, and Santiago). Service was curtailed in 2004 by the George W. Bush administration but eased by the Obama administration in January 2011.[39] Several congressmen have tried to roll back the easing of travel restrictions but thus far have been unsuccessful (see Sullivan 2012b).

Following the series of policy changes in 2011, charter service to and from Cuba was authorized from an additional 12 US airports, making a total of 15.[40] As of early 2012, a total of 19 airports were permitted to accommodate charter flights to the ten destinations specified as points of entry in Cuba.[41] In addition, the number of CSPs has expanded: Currently, around 30 charter operators hold CSP licenses.[42] Major airlines that operate flights for charter companies and hold CSP licenses include Delta, American, and United Airlines.[43]

Round trip fares for US flights to Cuba generally range from $400 to $600, varying by the charter location and time of year. For example, according to ABC Charters, a 45-minute round trip flight from Miami to Havana generally costs around $449 in most months of 2013 (the fare includes mandatory medical insurance and taxes), but the price rises to $589 in the high season (July to September).

---

39. A number of OFAC regulatory changes affecting travel restrictions occurred during the Bush administration. For more details, see Sullivan (2012a).

40. In January 2011, the US Department of Homeland Security published the final rule, "Airports of Entry or Departure for Flights to and from Cuba," which "allows additional US airports that are able to process international flights to request approval of the US Customs and Border Protection (CBP) to process authorized flights between the US and Cuba." See US CBP, "Approved U.S. Ports of Entry for Flights to and from Cuba," February 2, 2012, www.cbp.gov/xp/cgov/travel/travel_news. In addition to Miami International, Los Angeles International, and John F. Kennedy airports, newly authorized US airports in 2011 are Atlanta, Baltimore-Washington (BWI), Chicago O'Hare, Dallas-Fort Worth, Fort Lauderdale-Hollywood, Houston, New Orleans, Oakland (CA), Pittsburgh, San Juan (Puerto Rico), Southwest Florida International Airport (Fort Myers), and Tampa.

41. Flight entry and exit points in Cuba are specified in the US FAA's *International Flight Information Manual for Cuba*, www.faa.gov/air_traffic/publications/ifim.

42. See OFAC's list (as of January 2013) of authorized providers of air, travel, and remittance forwarding services to Cuba, www.treasury.gov/resource-center/sanctions/Programs/pages/Cuba. In addition, over 300 licensed travel service providers in the United States make commercial travel arrangements to Cuba, e.g., book flights and hotel reservations and provide other Cuba travel services.

43. See "Airlines Rev Up for Flights to Cuba," *Wall Street Journal*, October 24, 2011, http://online.wsj.com (accessed on March 21, 2013).

US Open Skies Agreements

According to a State Department fact sheet, Open Skies agreements are designed to "expand international passenger and cargo flights by eliminating government interference in commercial airline decisions about routes, capacity, and pricing. This frees carriers to provide more affordable, convenient, and efficient air service to consumers, promoting increased travel and trade, and spurring high-quality job opportunities and economic growth. The Open Skies policy rejects the outmoded practice of highly restrictive ASAs protecting flag carriers."[44] US Open Skies agreements allow air carriers unlimited market access to the markets of each partner and the right to fly to all intermediate points and beyond.

The United States has Open Skies agreements with over 100 countries from all regions of the world and at varying levels of economic development. Over 70 percent of international flights from the United States are to Open Skies partners.[45] Of the North American countries, Canada is an Open Skies partner but not Mexico. Instead US-Mexico aviation services are still governed by a bilateral ASA.

Cuban Air Services Agreements

Cuba has over 70 bilateral ASAs, including with Canada, the United States (dating from 1953), Spain, France, Italy, Brazil, China, and most countries in Latin America,[46] and Cuba concluded a multilateral air transport agreement in 2004 with the Association of Caribbean States. In 2010, Canada updated its bilateral ASA with Cuba through an "expanded" air services agreement, which, while distinct from an Open Skies agreement, allows "more airlines from both countries to immediately operate scheduled air services between any Canadian and Cuban cities."[47] Some European countries have negotiated similar arrangements with Cuba.

Cuban Aviation Sector

Cuba's aviation authority (analogous to the US Federal Aviation Administration [FAA]) is the Instituto de Aeronáutica Civil de Cuba (IACC), which was created in 1985 and belongs to key international bodies including the International Civil

44. US State Department, "Open Skies Partnerships: Expanding the Benefits of Freer Commercial Aviation," fact sheet, March 29, 2011, www.state.gov/r/pa/pl/159347.htm (accessed on March 19, 2013).

45. Ibid.

46. For a complete list, see IACC, "Acuerdos Bilaterales y Multilaterales de Transporte Aereo" ["Bilateral and Multilateral Air Transport Agreements"], www.iacc.gov.cu/tari.htm#politicatari.

47. Transport Canada, "Canada Announces More Air Travel Options in the Caribbean," press release no. H014/10, February 7, 2010, www.tc.gc.ca/eng/mediaroom/releases-2010-h014e-5823.htm (accessed on March 22, 2013).

Aviation Organization (ICAO), the International Air Transport Association (IATA), and the Latin American Civil Aviation Commission. The IACC is responsible for "directing, implementing and monitoring the policy of the State and the Government in regard to air transport, civil air navigation aids and related services."[48] Cuba has ten international airports, which, according to the IACC, handle more than 40 foreign airlines on scheduled flights and charters.[49] Cuba's airlines, all state-owned, include Cubana de Aviación (known as Cubana), Cuba's national airline and the largest, along with Aerocaribbean, Aerogaviota, and Aerotaxi, a charter airline.

There is no direct commercial air service to the United States by Cuban carriers and the US FAA has not assessed the IACC for compliance with ICAO safety standards.[50]

Impact of Sanctions on Air Travel

Cuba evaluated the impact of US sanctions on the Cuban civil aviation sector in a 2013 report to the ICAO. The report's conclusions include:

- The ban on Cuban airline companies from operating in the United States has had an enormous economic impact.[51]

- Based on specific cases, US sanctions have effectively impeded the modernization of automatic check-in and baggage systems;[52] prevented the supply of certain spare aircraft parts from third-country manufacturers; decreased Cubana's aviation internet sales due to North American visa restrictions; and impeded financial transfers from Cuban airlines to banks in third countries.

- The estimated impact on Cuba's civil aviation sector from 1960 to 2012 amounts to approximately $4 billion.

---

48. IACC, "Quienes Somos" ["About Us"], www.iacc.gov.cu (accessed on March 19, 2013).

49. IACC, "Breve reseña historia" ["Brief History"], www.iacc.gov.cu/historia.htm (accessed on March 22, 2013).

50. The US Interests Section in Havana instructs visitors "to avoid domestic or international travel on Cuban air carriers, including the Cuban national airline Cubana de Aviación, whenever possible due to serious concerns regarding Cuba's ability to meet international safety oversight standards." See US Department of State, "Cuba Country Specific Information," March 11, 2013, http://travel.state.gov/travel/cis_pa_tw/cis/cis_1097.html (accessed March 15, 2013).

51. Following the US embargo, the Cuban aviation sector was severely restricted in its access to supplies and spare parts. Cuban airplanes were initially supplied with these items from the Soviet Union. During the 1970s, Cubana leased Douglas DC-8s from Air Canada, in the 1990s McDonnell Douglas DC-10s from France, and in the mid-1990s Airbus A320s. See Smithsonian Air and Space Museum, "Cuban Aviation History," www.postalmuseum.si.edu/pichs/aviation/exhibit1.htm (accessed on March 15, 2013).

52. This claim seems exaggerated, since check-in systems and baggage handling equipment are available from European and Asian firms.

Potential US-Cuba Travel

According to the US Department of Transportation (DOT), the number of passengers on direct flights from the United States to Cuba has steadily increased over the past few years: There were nearly 196,000 passengers in 2009, 242,000 in 2010, 348,000 in 2011, and perhaps 390,000 in 2012 (based on eight-month figures).[53] These figures, moreover, do not count Americans who travel to Cuba through third countries, particularly Canada and Mexico.[54] Various estimates suggest that the overall number of US travelers to Cuba was around 400,000 in 2011, or about 15 percent larger than reported data (Sullivan 2012a, 16).

While these flows are significant, in the wake of economic normalization and an Open Skies agreement, travel to Cuba could be substantially larger. Traffic growth following the conclusion of a standard, bilateral ASA typically averaged between 12 and 35 percent, significantly greater than during the period preceding air services liberalization (InterVISTAS-ga 2006). A simulation of liberalizing 320 country pair markets not in Open Skies agreements (i.e., not yet deregulated) found a one-time gain in traffic of nearly 63 percent—dramatically higher than typical world traffic growth of around 6 to 8 percent annually (InterVISTAS-ga 2006).

Air traffic from the United States to the Caribbean islands remains substantial: In 2012, 6.4 million US tourists[55] traveled to the Caribbean with an average travel expenditure (excluding airfare) of $1,000 per person.[56] Easily an additional one million Americans per year could visit Cuba in the wake of complete normalization.[57] This influx of tourism activity could translate to roughly $1 billion in additional tourist receipts for Cuba.

---

53. Air carrier statistics are from US Department of Transportation, TranStats database, Research and Innovative Technology Administration, Bureau of Transportation Statistics, www.transtats. bts.gov/homepage.asp.

54. The overall number of travelers from the United States to Cuba could be somewhat inflated since some Cuban-Americans visiting family likely travel to Cuba more than once a year (Sullivan 2012a).

55. Based on figures released by the US Department of Commerce, Office of Travel & Tourism Industries, "U.S. Citizen Air Traffic to Overseas Regions," http://tinet.ita.doc.gov. The Caribbean Tourism Organization reports a higher estimate of 8.5 million US tourists to the Caribbean in 2012, but this figure also includes tourist arrivals for Belize, Cancún, Guyana, and Puerto Rico.

56. According to the US Bureau of Economic Analysis, total US travel expenditure (travel payments excluding passenger fares) to the Caribbean in 2012 was approximately $6.4 billion. Travel payments are the purchases of goods and services by Americans traveling abroad, e.g., food, lodging, recreation, gifts, entertainment, local transportation, etc.

57. According to Emilio Morales (2013), approximately three-quarters of current US travelers to Cuba are Cuban-Americans. The significant increase in tourism that we foresee with normalization assumes that other Americans, who customarily travel to other destinations in the Caribbean, will visit Cuba.

Reciprocity Measures

The potential spur to economic prosperity in Cuba from an Open Skies agreement would be substantial and should provide a major incentive for reciprocal concessions by the Cuban government. The United States should ease restriction on licensing for charter flights further. In return, Cuba should allow US air carriers unrestricted market access to Cuban airports. As an initial step the United States and Cuba could revisit their existing ASA and negotiate an expanded agreement to allow more airlines to operate scheduled air services to Cuba. The US FAA should assess Cuba's IACC for compliance with ICAO safety standards, which would allow Cuban airlines to operate scheduled air services to US cities.

Immigration and Professional Visas

Current US policy is focused on permanent immigration, driven primarily by political concerns rather than economic considerations. Cuban citizens can apply for admission to the United States as legal permanent residents (LPRs) through one of three channels: (1) family-based immigrant visa, (2) refugee resettlement, and (3) parole under the Special Cuban Migration Program (also known as the Cuban Lottery).

This system of immigration was developed through the Cuban Adjustment Act (CAA) of 1996 and the US-Cuba Migration Accords of 1994 and 1995. The CAA allows Cuban citizens who have been physically present in the United States for at least one year to claim LPR status, a right given solely to Cubans. Under the 1994 accord, the United States agreed to issue a minimum of 20,000 visas to Cubans annually. The accord also established the so-called wet foot/dry foot policy: Cubans arriving by land were permitted to stay in the United States, while those intercepted at sea were placed in a third country or a safe haven camp, which at the time was the US naval base in Guantanamo. The 1995 accord altered the wet foot/dry foot policy so that Cubans intercepted at sea were instead repatriated to Cuba. As part of the accord the Cuban government agreed not to penalize repatriated citizens, and the United States agreed to allow Cubans detained at Guantanamo to travel to the United States through the humanitarian parole provisions of the US Immigration and Nationality Act.[58] The 1995 accord also committed the United States and Cuba to hold semiannual talks on migration policy.

Talks were held for a decade before they were suspended by the United States in 2004, owing to Cuba's refusal to discuss key issues relevant to Cuban migration.[59] The talks resumed in 2009, and four rounds were held between

---

58. Typically humanitarian parole is used to bring otherwise inadmissible aliens into the United States temporarily. However, the 1966 CAA allows Cubans to adjust to permanent legal status and remain permanently in the United States.

59. The major issues included Cuba's exit visa program, Cuban restrictions related to US monitoring of repatriated Cubans, and Cuba's obligation to accept repatriated Cubans (Wasem 2009).

2009 and 2011 (Sullivan 2012b). Again they were halted because Cuba arrested a subcontractor of the US Agency for International Development (USAID). However, in 2013, the talks resumed. An immediate result is that nonimmigrant visas for Cuban travelers to the United States will now have a duration of five years rather than six months. Moreover, B-2 visas for family or personal travel will be allowed multiple entries.[60] Meanwhile, as mentioned earlier, Cuba has abolished its own exit permit requirements and liberalized its passport policy for the great majority of Cubans.

It remains to be seen how these changes will affect nonimmigrant Cubans working in the United States. In 2010, less than 1 percent of all visas issued to Cubans were employment-based (Wasem 2012). Once Cuba transitions to a democracy and bilateral relations normalize, the United States may further adjust its immigration policy toward Cubans, shifting the focus to economic considerations. For example, instead of emphasizing permanent immigration to the United States, US policy might promote greater temporary movement to the United States for education and employment purposes. This would allow Cubans to develop new skills and gain work experience that contributes to Cuban economic growth.

There are two nonimmigrant work visas that Cubans could take advantage of once bilateral relations are normalized: the professional work visa (H-1B) and the intracorporate transferee visa (L-1). The H-1B visa is for high-skilled foreign workers entering a "specialty occupation." To qualify for an H-1B visa the worker must have, at a minimum, a bachelor's degree or equivalent work experience. The drawback of the H-1B is its numerical cap. Unlike the preferential treatment given to Cubans under the current system of immigration, the H-1B does not provide country-based quotas or any favorable treatment related to existing bilateral trade or investment relations. The number of H-1B visas that may be issued annually has been capped by Congress at 85,000 persons, and 20,000 of those are reserved for individuals with a master's or higher degree from a US institution. In addition, all H-1B applicants must have an offer of employment to qualify for a visa.

The L-1 visa allows employees of a US company who have worked abroad for at least one year in a managerial or executive role to work at a branch, parent, affiliate, or subsidiary of that company in the United States. The L-1 visa is appealing because it is not limited by any quota. Also, as economic relations between the United States and Cuba strengthen and US firms begin to invest in Cuba, Cubans will be able to take advantage of the L-1 visa.

The United States might also consider creating a special category of visas for Cubans that would allow them to bypass the H-1B quota. In past years, the United States has created special categories of visas for select countries through provisions in an FTA. For example, the North American Free Trade Agreement (NAFTA) created the NAFTA Professional (TN) visa, which allows

---

60. See "US Ups Duration Of Non-Immigrant Visas For Cubans," Associated Press, July 31, 2013, www.npr.org/templates/story/story.php?storyId=207341045 (accessed on September 7, 2013).

Canadians and Mexicans to work temporarily in the United States in one of a list of designated professions (e.g., accounting, engineering, sciences, etc.). Similarly, the US-Singapore FTA established the H-1B1 visa that provides similar employment opportunities for professional Singaporeans. In the case of Cuba, the United States could create a new class of nonimmigrant work visa through the existing program that allocates a minimum of 20,000 visas annually for Cubans. These visas have historically been allocated through family-based immigration or refugee resettlement programs. However, the United States could allocate a certain percentage of the existing quota to nonimmigrant work visas, or it could expand the quota for skilled and professional applicants.

Reciprocity Measures

A special visa category for Cubans might be possible over the medium term—provided, of course, that political normalization is solidly grounded. As a precursor, Cuba should further relax its restrictions on the movement of people. Cuba has taken some initial steps in this direction, by announcing, in October 2012, that it would eliminate the exit permit required by Cubans to travel abroad. Additionally, the government announced that Cubans would be allowed to stay abroad for up to 24 months. Previously, Cubans were required to obtain an exit permit to travel overseas and could remain abroad for a maximum of 11 months without losing their citizenship rights. The new policy also removes the long-standing restriction on the movement of healthcare professionals, who, in the past, were routinely denied exit permits. The new policy came into effect on January 14, 2013, and marks the first time in over 50 years that Cuba has reformed its travel and immigration policy.[61] Travel abroad still requires Cubans to obtain a passport, and the government still has the right to deny passports to its citizens and maintains restrictions for certain "strategic" occupations such as those related to national security.[62] Yet on balance the Cuban policy for citizens wishing to travel abroad has been significantly liberalized.

Offshore Oil and Gas Exploration

Cuba has a relatively small oil and gas industry. Based on the latest available data, in 2012 Cuba produced 51,000 barrels of oil per day, making the country the 61st producer in the world. Cuba is ranked 64 in terms of proven oil reserves, which were estimated to be 0.1 billion barrels in 2013 (EIA 2013). Domestic production is not sufficient to meet domestic consumption, which in 2010

---

61. Travel and immigration policy was last reformed in 1961, when Fidel Castro initiated travel restrictions to prevent Cuban professionals from leaving the country.

62. Nick Miroff, "After 50 Years, Cuba Drops Unpopular Travel Restriction," NPR, January 11, 2013, www.npr.org/2013/01/11/169070431/after-50-years-cuba-drops-unpopular-travel-restriction (accessed on May 14, 2013).

Table 7.2 Overview of Cuba's oil and gas sector

Fuel type	Reserves	Production	Consumption	Exports	Imports
	(billions of barrels/day)		(thousands of barrels/day)		
Crude oil	0.1	50.8	n.a.	0	120.1
Refined petroleum products	n.a.	100.6	163.9	11.3	4.9
	Reserves	Production	Consumption	Exports	Imports
		(billion cubic feet)			
Natural gas	2,500	36	36	0	0

n.a. = not applicable

Note: Figures based on the latest year of available data. Data for crude oil and natural gas reserves areas of 2013. All other data for crude oil are from 2012 and for natural gas from 2011. All data for refined petroleum products are from 2010.

Source: US Energy Information Administration, *International Energy Statistics*, 2013, www.eia.gov/countries/data.cfm.

was 164,000 barrels per day (table 7.2). Cuba therefore relies on imports, which consist mainly of refined petroleum products like kerosene, distillate fuel oil, liquefied petroleum gases, and other products. Almost all oil consumption is used for heat and electric power, with a small portion for transportation. Cuba's only oil exports consist of refined products, mainly motor gasoline and jet fuel. Cuba is ranked 56th in the world for proven natural gas reserves, which were estimated to be 2.5 trillion cubic feet as of 2013 (table 7.2). Cuba produces small amounts of natural gas, 36 billion cubic feet in 2011, used entirely for domestic consumption.

Despite the small level of domestic production, significant opportunities exist for FDI in the oil and gas sector. The proven reserves reported by the US Energy Information Administration are located onshore or near shore in shallow waters and have been the focus of current production and exploration. The US Geological Survey, however, estimates that the offshore waters of the North Cuba Basin could contain an *additional* 4.6 billion barrels of oil and 9.8 trillion cubic feet of natural gas (Schenk 2010).

Tapping reserves in the North Cuba Basin would require deepwater drilling for which Cuba does not have the necessary technology. A number of foreign energy companies have signed contracts with Cuba to explore offshore reserves. In 2004, Spain's Repsol YPF, S.A. (renamed Repsol, S.A. in May 2012) drilled Cuba's first and only deepwater well. Repsol YPF deemed the well not commercially viable and did not move forward with development (Nerurkar and Sullivan 2011). More recently, the Cuban government signed contracts with foreign energy companies to lease blocks of its North Basin. Table 7.3 summarizes these investments. Other companies, like Russia's state-owned Zarubezhneft, have contracts to explore the shallower waters. The largest investment is a joint venture between Repsol YPF (40 percent), Norway's Statoil (30 percent), and India's Oil and Natural Gas Corporation (ONGC) (30 percent) to explore six blocks. Despite the recent influx of FDI, oil exploration has been extremely slow and several companies have failed to find commercially viable oil wells.

One of the main obstacles to oil and gas exploration in Cuba's ultradeep waters is the extremely high cost of drilling. US sanctions prohibit US companies from investing or engaging in commercial activity with the Cuban government or any Cuban entity. US sanctions also prohibit the use in Cuba of technology or equipment with more than 10 percent US content. Since the United States leads much of the technology and equipment used in deepwater oil and gas industry, it is difficult for foreign companies to acquire the necessary equipment. Currently there is only one ultra-deep-water oil platform that contains less than 10 percent US content: Scarabeo 9, owned by the Italian company Saipem, was built in China and outfitted in Singapore and towed across the Pacific Ocean to Cuba. The high cost of constructing and transporting Scarabeo 9 plus the fact that it is the only ultra-deep-water platform in the world that can drill in Cuba without violating US sanctions make it extremely expensive to lease. At an estimated $500,000 per day, only three companies have leased the Scarabeo 9. In 2012, Repsol YPF, Petroleos de Venezuela, S.A., and Malaysia's Petronas used the deepwater platform to drill

Table 7.3   Foreign direct investment in Cuba's offshore oil

Country	Company	Number of blocks leased
Angola	Sonangol	2
China	National Petroleum Corporation	5
India	Oil and Natural Gas Corporation[a]	8
Malaysia	Petronas[b]	4
Norway	Statoil[a]	6
Russia	Gazprom[b]	4
Spain	Repsol YPF[a]	6
Venezuela	Petroleos de Venezuela, S.A.	4
Vietnam	PetroVietnam	4

a. Repsol YPF, Oil and Natural Gas Corporation, and Statoil have a joint venture to explore six blocks.
b. Petronas and Gazprom are in a joint venture to develop four blocks.

Source: Nerurkar and Sullivan (2011).

exploratory wells.[63] Although some wells did contain oil, none were deemed commercially viable to produce and the companies did not engage in further drilling. In late 2012, Scarabeo 9 departed Cuban waters for Africa, leaving the country without the equipment necessary for further exploration. Most recently, Zarubezhneft is using the Norwegian-owned shallow water plat-form—the Songa Mercur—to drill exploratory wells. Like the Scarabeo 9, the Songa Mercur meets the US requirements of less than 10 percent US content. However, the Songa Mercur only has the capacity to drill in shallow water, around 1,000 feet, unlike the Scarabeo 9, which can drill to depths of 12,000 feet and is capable of exploring the more lucrative blocks in the northern and western waters of Cuba.

Cuba's natural gas also offers opportunities. It is found in crude oil reservoirs and could be developed along with crude oil found in Cuba's North Basin and western waters in the Gulf of Mexico, where natural gas reserves are estimated to be 2.5 trillion cubic feet. Currently, natural gas represents a small fraction of Cuba's total energy consumption. According to the International Energy Agency (IEA), the industrial sector accounts for about 83 percent of natural gas consumption, while the residential sector accounts for about 16 percent.[64] The Canadian mining company Sherritt International has a large

63. David LaGesse, "Cuba's Oil Quest to Continue, Despite Deepwater Disappointment," *National Geographic News*, November 19, 2012, http://news.nationalgeographic.com (accessed on April 8, 2013).

64. "Cuba: Natural Gas for 2011," IEA statistics, www.iea.org/statistics/statisticssearch/report/?country=CUBA&product=naturalgas&year=Select (accessed on December 19, 2013).

stake in Cuba's natural gas production. The company entered into a joint venture with state-run Cubapetroleo (CUPET) in the early 1990s to produce natural gas for electricity generation. However, Sherritt International does not possess the technology and equipment for deepwater drilling.

Once relations with the United States are normalized, the potential for oil and gas exploration in Cuban waters will substantially improve. Access to US technology and the elimination of content requirements for equipment will make exploration and production much more viable. What's more, US companies will have the opportunity to invest in Cuba's oil and gas industry. Participating in the development of Cuba's reserves is in the US interest for two reasons. First, given the geographical proximity of Cuba, the United States should be concerned about the safe and environmentally sound development of deepwater oil and gas. Second, increasing domestic production of oil and gas will help Cuba reduce its dependence on imports from Venezuela.

Cuba currently imports the majority of its oil from Venezuela, through the bilateral comprehensive cooperation agreement that allows Cuba to purchase oil at favorable prices. Cuba and Venezuela signed their bilateral agreement in October 2000, which committed Venezuela to supply Cuba with an estimated 90,000 to 130,000 barrels per day. As part of the agreement 60 percent of Cuba's oil purchases are paid in the form of goods and services—mainly medical doctors, pharmaceutical products, teachers, and sports trainers. The remaining 40 percent of oil purchases are paid through long-term financing (over 25 years), at favorable prices and interest rates (Feinberg 2011).

Reciprocity Measures

Cuba should give US firms equal footing in the oil and gas sector, allowing them to invest through joint ventures and wholly owned companies. In exchange, the United States should eliminate the content requirements that currently restrict the use of technology and equipment essential to deepwater exploration. The United States has a near monopoly on this technology and Cuba is severely limited by the restrictions currently imposed.

Another area of cooperation relates to prevention and remediation of oil spills, which is a major US concern following the Deepwater Horizon oil spill in the Gulf of Mexico. The United States has taken initial steps toward preparedness. For example, it has licensed US companies to provide equipment and services required in case of a spill. Cuba should reciprocate by engaging in direct government-to-government dialogue to develop a joint preparedness plan.

Sanitary and Phytosanitary and Technical Barriers to Trade Regulations

Cuba is a net food importer and represents a lucrative export market for US agricultural goods. Geographic proximity and the low cost of US agricultural production make the United States an ideal supplier to the Cuban market. In

2000, the United States reformed its sanctions program through the Trade Sanctions Reform and Export Enhancement Act (TSRA), which authorized certain agricultural products to be exported to Cuba provided that Cuban purchases are paid in cash and not credit. Despite these reforms, US agricultural exports to Cuba remain negligible—just over $400 million in 2011 and flat over the past decade. Corn, meat (poultry and some pork), and soybeans account for over 75 percent of total US agricultural exports.

Technical barriers to trade (TBT), as well as sanitary and phytosanitary (SPS) provisions, are a major obstacle to two-way trade. The United States restricts visits by Cuban nationals to the United States for SPS inspections of US products and processing facilities, making it extremely difficult for Cuban and US suppliers to negotiate procurement contracts. The Empresa Cubana Comercializadora de Alimentos (Alimport) is the government body authorized to import agricultural products from the United States.[65] Alimport is charged with arranging supply contracts and carrying out logistics for Cuban imports. The Cuban Ministry of Agriculture issues SPS permits to importers, required before any sales contract can be executed. In addition, US exporters must register their company with the Cuban Ministry of Agriculture and register their products with the Institute of Nutrition and Food Safety. Registration requires samples of the product in question. Additionally, Cuba requires that a Cuban government official inspect import products at their source, and in the case of meat products this requires inspection of the farm or processing facility. US restrictions on Cuban travel to the United States make inspections difficult to coordinate. In addition, the financing requirements for sales contracts are extremely complex due to restrictions imposed by sanctions.

Normalization of US-Cuba relations and subsequent easing of travel and financing restrictions will facilitate bilateral agricultural trade. According to the US Department of Agriculture's Animal and Plant Health Inspection Services (APHIS), Cuba's SPS system is generally consistent with international norms and is not likely to present significant barriers to US agricultural exports (USITC 2007). For example, Cuba's protocols for genetically modified rice, grain, and oilseed imports from the United States are considered to be "reasonable...and based upon sound science" (FAS/USDA 2008, 26). In the early 2000s, Cuba developed a new food safety program that includes surveillance, inspection, education, training, and standardization. Cuba is also a member of the WTO's SPS and TBT agreements. Cuba has not been party to any WTO dispute concerning SPS issues and has been an active participant in the operation and implementation of the SPS and TBT agreements. Cuba has a technical working group that serves as the national enquiry point of contact for the SPS and TBT committees and analyzes and circulates WTO recommendations. In partnership with other Caribbean countries, Cuba sub-

---

65. While the United States is required to export agricultural products to Alimport only, other countries are permitted to sell their products directly to Cuban state-owned enterprises.

mitted a proposal—approved in 2006—to the WTO's Committee on Trade and Development (CTD), which allows regional bodies to assist small economies in the implementation of their obligations in the SPS and TBT agreements.[66]

Reciprocity Measures

Despite Cuba's seemingly comprehensive SPS system, there will undoubtedly be barriers to expanded agricultural trade. Given stringent US SPS and TBT rules and regulations, Cuba will likely require some assistance in the harmonization of provisions, and the United States should play an active role in providing technical assistance. The SPS provisions included in the Central American Free Trade Agreement–Dominican Republic (CAFTA-DR) provide a useful precedent. The FTA established SPS and TBT committees and, for the first time, included a trade capacity building chapter that worked in coordination with the committees to assist in the implementation and conformity of SPS and TBT procedures. The SPS committee identified "regional SPS priorities" for CAFTA-DR countries. These included the development of risk assessment methodologies, upgrading of laboratory infrastructure, and strengthening of national WTO/SPS enquiry points. US government agencies provided financial support and technical assistance to the CAFTA-DR countries to bring their SPS and TBT regulations in line with US and international standards.

The United States should consider initiating a similar partnership with the Cuban government to facilitate the harmonization of standards and avoid unnecessary delays in moving agricultural products. In return Cuba should undertake reforms that allow US agricultural producers to expand and diversify their market share in Cuba.

Free Trade Agreement

Once Cuba has enacted political and economic reforms conducive to a free market economy, the United States might consider deepening commercial relations through a bilateral FTA. An FTA would consolidate and augment trade and investment preferences extended to Cuba under any prior bilateral agreements, such as a TIFA or BIT. More importantly, an FTA would further strengthen bilateral economic relations, stimulate growth, and provide a platform for further cooperation.

For the United States, crafting an FTA with Cuba would give US companies additional opportunities to participate in the economic development of

---

66. For the complete text of the proposal submitted to the WTO CTD, see "Agreement on the Application of Sanitary and Phytosanitary Measures: Designation of a Regional Body," Communication from Antigua and Barbuda, Barbados, Cuba, Dominica, Fiji, Grenada, Jamaica, Mauritius, Papua New Guinea, Solomon Islands, St. Kitts and Nevis, St. Vincent and the Grenadines, WT/COMTD/SE/W/16/Rev.1 & Rev.2, April 10, 2006, available at www.wto.org/english/news_e/news06_e/sps_june06_e.htm.

Cuba, through both trade and investment. US interest will be focused on increasing agricultural exports, investing in Cuba's tourism industry, oil and gas exploration, and potentially Cuba's agribusiness and medical services sectors. For Cuba, an FTA with the United States would mean greater access to low-cost agricultural goods, higher-quality services, and much-needed technology and training.

The economic payoffs of an FTA would be substantial. Based on the results of our gravity model estimates discussed in chapter 6, and summarized in tables 6.2 and 6.3, an FTA between the United States and Cuba would give a big boost to bilateral trade flows. Current trade flows are minimal: US merchandise exports to Cuba are hovering around $400 million, while Cuban merchandise exports to the United States are near zero. Under economic normalization, potential bilateral merchandise trade flows would be $4.3 billion of US exports and $5.8 billion of Cuban exports.[67] If the United States and Cuba concluded an FTA, however, potential trade might increase by nearly 88 percent, with just over $8 billion in US merchandise exports to Cuba and nearly $11 billion in Cuban merchandise exports to the United States (see table 6.2).

Reciprocity Measures

Negotiating a bilateral FTA would be extremely challenging and is unlikely to occur in the medium term. The Cuban government has indicated its intention to transition more economic activity from the state to the private sector over the next four to five years, with the private sector eventually accounting for roughly 45 percent of GDP (Sullivan 2012b, 26). But this will require deep and comprehensive reforms. Before the United States considers a bilateral FTA, Cuba will also have to upgrade its labor standards. If an FTA is eventually negotiated, it will entail reciprocal concessions between Cuban firms (whether private or state-owned) and private US firms. For the United States, it will be important not to fully open its market to Cuba unilaterally, before Cuba has implemented or is willing to undertake crucial reforms. Otherwise, in our view, the Cuban authorities will have little reason to negotiate a meaningful FTA.

CAFTA-DR could serve as a model for a bilateral US-Cuba FTA. The agreement includes an extended tariff phaseout schedule, safeguard measures, and a number of capacity-building measures to assist the CAFTA countries with the transition and bring their trade practices in line with US and international standards.

CAFTA-DR delayed the duty-free treatment of certain products deemed the most sensitive and included separate provisions for specific goods. For example, duties on some US nontextile and manufactured goods were phased out over a period of up to 10 years, while for other products duty-free treatment did not even start for seven or more years after the agreement was imple-

---

67. For a discussion of likely trade flows under economic normalization, see chapter 6.

mented (Hornbeck 2012). It is likely that the United States would invoke some of these longer phaseout periods, together with special terms for certain goods, notably sugar. Under CAFTA-DR, the United States agreed to increase its sugar quota by 2 percent each year, in perpetuity, but did not agree to decrease the above-quota tariff rate (USTR 2004).

Another important element of CAFTA-DR that could serve as a model for a US-Cuba agreement is the capacity building provision. The FTA includes a separate chapter on trade capacity building focused on helping CAFTA countries implement the provisions of the FTA, through technical assistance, training, and joint cooperation. For example, the United States, through USAID and USDA, has funded technical assistance and training to develop electronic export windows in CAFTA countries. Joint initiatives have also included investment in laboratory infrastructure and harmonizing risk assessment tools to bring SPS systems up to US and international standards (USTR 2007). The international financial institutions (International Monetary Fund, World Bank, and Inter-American Development Bank) also played a large role in CAFTA-DR capacity building and could play a similar role in Cuba, which will undoubtedly require technical and financial assistance to update its hard and soft infrastructure.

8

US Offensive and Defensive Interests

American trade negotiators often speak of "offensive" and "defensive" interests, meaning concessions they want and concessions they might give. The largest US "offensive" interest, of course, is Cuba's transition from a state-run economy and autocratically governed country to a democratically governed market economy. Unless Cuban leaders and people welcome this transition it will not happen. Optimistically, we think the transition has already begun, though at a very gradual pace. Realistically, we think the transition will continue on a gradual path, not as a big bang. Our evaluation of US offensive and defensive interests is couched within this forecast, first listing changes that the United States might offer as enticements for Cuban reform, and second listing changes that the United States might want to ensure an orderly transition and appropriate US participation in the Cuban economy. Since the potential changes have been previewed in earlier chapters, here we simply summarize the possible economic menu. We emphasize again that substantial political normalization is the precondition for exploring this economic menu.

What Can the United States Offer Cuba?

The United States can table a long list of potential concessions, beginning with measures to unwind the embargo and possibly concluding (a decade or more later) with deep economic integration. However, in our view it is essential that each US concession be matched by a Cuban concession of roughly equivalent value.

- The United States could permit Cuba to join the International Monetary Fund (IMF), World Bank, and Inter-American Development Bank and allow those institutions to offer technical assistance to Cuba.

- At a later juncture, the United States could accept that the international financial institutions will offer grants and loans to Cuba.
- The United States could gradually relax its restrictions on pleasure tourism, particularly the daily allowance of permitted expenditures.
- Likewise, the United States could gradually enlarge the range of goods and services that can be freely exported to Cuba, starting with food and household necessities and a range of business services.
- The United States could explore the possibility of encouraging aspects of medical tourism, including Medicare and Medicaid programs.
- The United States could open talks with Cuban officials on a trade and investment framework agreement, perhaps leading to a bilateral investment treaty (BIT). In this context, the United States could allow US firms to invest in Cuba, and vice versa, fostering bilateral trade.
- The United States could offer Cuba a full Open Skies agreement, coupled with technical assistance to meet Federal Aviation Administration safety standards.
- The United States could offer Cuba technical assistance for meeting US sanitary and phytosanitary standards for agricultural goods and relevant standards for manufactured products.
- The United States could enlarge the annual quota for Cuban immigrants and explore the recognition (on a reciprocal basis) of certain professional credentials.[1]
- Much later, when a democratic market economy was established in Cuba, the United States could welcome an initiative from Cuba to negotiate a free trade agreement.

What Can Cuba Offer the United States?

- Cuba can start by opening negotiations to settle expropriation claims, exploring a range of alternative settlement methods.
- Essential for creating a market economy and curbing corruption is to unify the exchange rate and establish an independent central bank. The IMF can provide valuable assistance for these critical reforms.
- As a matter of law and practice, Cuba could import US goods and services on the same basis as products from other countries (the most favored nation [MFN] principle, applied both de jure and de facto).
- As a matter of law and practice, Cuba can open investment opportunities

---

1. The quota of 20,000 immigrants annually, guaranteed under the Immigration Accord of 1994, implies an additional 200,000 Cuban immigrants over the next decade. Keeping the total the same, the rate of intake could be increased in the early years as part of a larger reconciliation program.

to US firms on the same terms extended to Canadian, European, Mexican, and other foreign firms (again MFN).

- Later, in the context of a BIT, Cuba could guarantee US firms the same rights and privileges as Cuban firms, including Cuban state-owned enterprises (the national treatment principle).

- Cuba could settle outstanding trademark disputes (Havana Club and Cohiba) on terms favorable to US interests.

- Cuba could lease ocean blocks to US firms for oil and gas exploration.

- Cuba could embark on a path of gradual and orderly privatization of its state-owned enterprises.

Sequencing "Gives" and "Gets"

When the moment arrives to embark on economic normalization, skilled American and Cuban negotiators will have their own ideas as to the proper sequence. So will political and economic constituencies in both countries. The order of policy changes scheduled in the two preceding sections broadly sketches what we regard as a sensible sequence of concessions. More precision from academic observers is probably not useful.

We conclude with the strong recommendation that, from the standpoint of US interests, economic normalization must be seen as a reciprocal process. If, instead, the United States offers most of its economic concessions in the immediate aftermath of political normalization we foresee two unfortunate results. First, Cuba's economic normalization will likely proceed at a slower pace, accompanied by greater favoritism to vested interests and greater corruption of public officials. Second, US firms and citizens will be pushed to the back of the line for commercial opportunities in Cuba.

References

Akhtar, Shayerah Ilias, Mary Jane Bolle, and Rebecca M. Nelson. 2013. *U.S. Trade and Investment in the Middle East and North Africa: Overview and Issues for Congress*. CRS Report to Congress R42153 (March 4). Washington: Congressional Research Service.

Anderson, James E. 1979. A Theoretical Foundation for the Gravity Equation. *American Economic Review* 69, no. 1: 106–16.

Anderson, James E., and Eric van Wincoop. 2003. Gravity with Gravitas: A Solution to the Border Puzzle. *American Economic Review* 93, no. 1: 170–92.

Anillo-Badia, Rolando. 2011. Outstanding Claims to Expropriated Property in Cuba. *Cuba in Transition* 21: 83–96. Papers and Proceedings of the Twenty-First Annual Meeting. Miami: Association for the Study of the Cuban Economy.

Åslund, Anders. 1992. *Post-Communist Economic Revolutions: How Big a Bang?* CSIS Significant Issues Series. Washington: Center for Strategic and International Studies.

Åslund, Anders. 2013. *How Capitalism Was Built: The Transformation of Central and Eastern Europe, Russia, and Central Asia*. Cambridge: Cambridge University Press.

Backer, Larry Catá, and Augusto I. Molina. 2009. Globalizing Cuba: ALBA and the Construction of Socialist Global Trade Systems. *Cuba in Transition* 19: 195–219. Papers and Proceedings of the Nineteenth Annual Meeting. Miami: Association for the Study of the Cuban Economy.

Bergstrand, J. H. 1985. The Gravity Equation in International Trade: Some Microeconomic Foundations and Empirical Evidence. *Review of Economic Statistics* 67, no. 3: 474–80.

Carter, Barry E. 2008. *International Economic Sanctions: Improving the Haphazard U.S. Legal Regime*. Cambridge, UK: Cambridge University Press.

Coleman, Jonathan R. 2001. The Economic Impact of U.S. Sanctions with Respect to Cuba. *Cuba in Transition* 11: 86–96. Papers and Proceedings of the Eleventh Annual Meeting. Miami: Association for the Study of the Cuban Economy.

Council of the Americas and Americas Society. 2013. *7 Steps the U.S. President Can Take to Promote Change in Cuba by Adapting the Embargo*. Policy Paper. Available at www.as-coa.org/sites/default/files/CWG7StepsMemo.pdf (accessed on December 11, 2013).

Deardorff, Alan V. 1998. Determinants of Bilateral Trade: Does Gravity Work in a Neoclassical World? In *The Regionalization of the World Economy*, ed. Jeffrey A. Frankel. Chicago: University of Chicago Press.

Deinard, Lile, and Amy Stasik. 2006. The Famous Marks Doctrine Under the Paris Convention: Is the Remedy Available to Foreign Entities in the Second Circuit? *New York Law Journal* (October 16). Available at www.dorsey.com/files/tbl_s13news/pdf95/2690/deinhard_stasik1006.pdf (accessed on April 28, 2013).

Deloitte Development LLC. 2008. *Medical Tourism: Consumers in Search of Value*. Washington: Deloitte Center for Health Solutions. Available at www.deloitte.com/assets/Dcom-united-States/Local%20Assets/Documents/us_chs_MedicalTourismStudy(3).pdf.

DeRosa, Dean A. 2007. *International Trade and Investment Data Set by 1-Digit SITC, 1976-2005*. Washington: Peterson Institute for International Economics.

DeRosa, Dean A. 2009. Morocco's Economic Performance under the FTA. In *Capitalizing on the Morocco-US Free Trade Agreement: A Road Map for Success*, ed. Gary C. Hufbauer and Claire Brunel. Washington: Peterson Institute for International Economics.

Di Bella, Gabriel, and Andy Wolfe. 2008. A Primer on Currency Unification and Exchange Rate Policy in Cuba: Lessons from Exchange Rate Unification in Transition Economies. *Cuba in Transition* 18: 354–67. Papers and Proceedings of the Eighteenth Annual Meeting. Miami: Association for the Study of the Cuban Economy.

Domínguez, Jorge. 2004. Cuba's Economic Transition: Successes, Deficiencies, and Challenges. In *The Cuban Economy at the Start of the Twenty-First Century*, ed. Jorge Domínguez, Omar Everleny Pérez Villanueva, and Lorena Barberia. Cambridge, MA: Harvard University Press.

Domínguez, Jorge I., Omar Everleny Pérez Villanueva, Mayra Espina Prieto, and Lorena Barberia, eds. 2012. *Cuban Economic and Social Development: Policy Reforms and Challenges in the 21st Century* (March). Cambridge, MA: Harvard University Press.

Drury, A. Cooper. 2000. How and Whom the US President Sanctions: A Time-Series—Cross-Section Analysis of US Sanction Decisions and Characteristics. In *Sanctions as Economic Statecraft: Theory and Practice*, ed. Steve Chan and A. Cooper Drury. London: Macmillan.

Echevarría, Oscar A. 1995. Cuba and the International Sugar Market. *Cuba in Transition* 5: 363–73. Papers and Proceedings of the Fifth Annual Meeting. Miami: Association for the Study of the Cuban Economy.

ECLAC (Economic Commission for Latin America and the Caribbean). 2011. *Foreign Direct Investment in Latin America and the Caribbean 2010*. Santiago: United Nations Economic Commission for Latin America and the Caribbean.

EIA (Energy Information Administration). 2013. Energy Statistics: Petroleum and Natural Gas. Washington.

Eichengreen, Barry, and Douglas A. Irwin. 1998. The Role of History in Bilateral Trade Flows. In *The Regionalization of the World Economy*. NBER Chapters. Cambridge, MA: National Bureau of Economic Research.

EIU (Economist Intelligence Unit). 2008. *Country Profile: Cuba*. London.

EIU (Economist Intelligence Unit). 2013. *Cuba Country Report* (August). London.

Erikson, Daniel P. 2009. *The Cuba Wars: Fidel Castro, the United States and the Next Revolution*. New York: Bloomsbury Press.

European Commission. 2010. *Cuba Country Strategy Paper and National Indicative Programme for the Period 2011–2013* (March). Available at http://ec.europa.eu.

Falk, Pamela S. 1998. Visions of Embargo Falling Spark U.S.-Cuba IP Battles. *National Law Journal* 20, no. 32 (April).

FAS/USDA (Foreign Agricultural Service, US Department of Agriculture). 2008. *Cuba's Food and Agriculture Situation Report* (March). Washington: Office of Global Analysis. Available at www. fas.usda.gov/itp/cuba/CubaSituation0308.pdf.

Feinberg, Richard E. 2011. *Reaching Out: Cuba's New Economy and the International Response* (November). Washington: Brookings Institution.

Feinberg, Richard E. 2012. *The New Cuban Economy: What Roles for Foreign Investment?* (December). Washington: Brookings Institution.

Feinberg, Richard E. 2013. *Soft Landing in Cuba? Emerging Entrepreneurs and Middle Classes.* Washington: Brookings Institution.

GAO (US Government Accountability Office). 2013. *Cuba Democracy Assistance: USAID's Program Is Improved, but State Could Better Monitor Its Implementing Partners.* Report to Chairman, Committee on Foreign Relations, US Senate, GAO 13-285 (January). Washington.

Gavin, Joseph G. 1989. Economic Sanctions: Foreign Policy Levers or Signals? *Policy Analysis*, no. 14 (November): 1–12.

Gershman, Carl, and Orlando Gutiérrez. 2009. Can Cuba Change? *Journal of Democracy* 20, no. 1 (January).

Gjelten, Tom. 2009. *Bacardi and the Long Fight for Cuba: The Biography of a Cause.* New York: Penguin Books.

Goldstein, Morris, and Mohsin Khan. 1985. Income and Price Effects in Foreign Trade. In *Handbook of International Economics* 2, ed. P. B. Kenen and R. W. Jones. Amsterdam: North-Holland.

González Gutiérrez, Alfredo. 1997. La economía sumergida en Cuba. In *Economía y reforma económica en Cuba*, ed. Dietmar Dirmoser and Jaime Estay. Caracas: Editorial Nueva Sociedad.

Henken, Ted. 2005. Entrepreneurship, Informality and the Second Economy: Cuba's Underground Economy in Comparative Perspective. *Cuba in Transition* 15: 88–101. Papers and Proceedings of the Fifteenth Annual Meeting. Miami: Association for the Study of the Cuban Economy.

Hernández-Catá, Ernesto. 2012. The Growth of the Cuban Economy in the First Decade of the XXI Century: Is It Sustainable? *Cuba in Transition* 22. Papers and Proceedings of the Twenty-Second Annual Meeting. Miami: Association for the Study of the Cuban Economy.

Hernández-Catá, Ernesto. 2013. *Cuba's Dependence on Venezuelan Assistance: A Quantitative Assessment.* Available at http://thecubaneconomy.com.

Hornbeck, J. F. 2012. *The Dominican Republic-Central America-United States Free Trade Agreement (CAFTA-DR): Developments in Trade and Investment.* CRS Report to Congress R42468 (April 9). Washington: Congressional Research Service.

HSBC. 2012. *Golf's 2020 Vision: The HSBC Report.* Prepared for HSBC by the Futures Company. Available at http://thefuturescompany.com/wp-content/uploads/2012/09/The_Future_of_Golf.pdf.

Hufbauer, Gary Clyde, and Christopher Findlay, eds. 1996. *Flying High: Liberalizing Civil Aviation in the Asia Pacific* (November). Washington: Institute for International Economics.

Hufbauer, Gary Clyde, Jeffrey J. Schott, and Kimberly Elliott. 1990. *Economic Sanctions Reconsidered*, 2d ed. Washington: Institute for International Economics.

Hufbauer, Gary Clyde, Jeffrey J. Schott, Kimberly Elliott, and Barbara Oegg. 2007. *Economic Sanctions Reconsidered*, 3d ed. Washington: Peterson Institute for International Economics.

ICAO (International Civil Aviation Organization). 2013. *Impact of the United States Economic, Commercial, and Financial Embargo against Cuba in the Civil Aviation Sector.* Working Paper ATConf/6-WP/37 prepared by Cuba for the Worldwide Air Transport Conference, Sixth Meeting, Montreal, March 18–22. Available at www.icao.int/Meetings/atconf6.

Ilias, Shayerah, and Ian F. Fergusson. 2011. *Intellectual Property Rights and International Trade.* CRS Report to Congress RL34292 (February 17). Washington: Congressional Research Service.

InterVISTAS-ga. 2006. *The Economic Impact of Air Services Liberalization*. Available at www.intervistas. com/downloads/Economic_Impact_of_Air_Service_Liberalization_Final_Report.pdf (accessed on December 11, 2013).

Javorcik, Beata S., and Shang-Jin Wei. 2009. Corruption and Cross-Border Investment in Emerging Markets: Firm-Level Evidence. *Journal of International Money and Finance* 28, no. 4: 605–24.

Johnson, Lise. 2012. The 2012 US Model BIT and What the Changes (or Lack Thereof) Suggest About Future Investment Treaties. *Political Risk Insurance Newsletter* (November). Available at www.vcc.columbia.edu.

Jones, Vivian. 2013. *Generalized System of Preferences: Background and Renewal Debate*. CRS Report to Congress RL33663 (July 24). Washington: Congressional Research Service.

Kaempfer, William H., and Anton D. Lowenberg. 1988. The Theory of International Economic Sanctions: A Public Choice Approach. *American Economic Review* 78 (September): 786–93.

Kimmerling, Stephen J. 1999. Havana Club: A Case Summary and an Analysis of Selected Legal Issues. *Cuba in Transition* 9: 120–40. Papers and Proceedings of the Ninth Annual Meeting. Miami: Association for the Study of the Cuban Economy.

KPMG International. 2011. Sharing Knowledge on Topical Issues in the Healthcare Sector. *Issues Monitor* 7 (May). Available at www.kpmg.com/CH/en/Library/Articles-Publications/Documents/Sectors/pub-20120207-issues-monitor-healthcare-medical-tourism-en.pdf.

Laverty, Collin. 2009. *Cuba's New Resolve: Economic Reform and Its Implications for US Policy*. Washington: Center for Democracy in the Americas.

Lee, Brianna. 2012. *The Organization of American States*. New York: Council on Foreign Relations.

Lee, Margaret Mikyung. 2004. *Restricting Trademark Rights of Cubans: WTO Decision and Congressional Response*. CRS Report to Congress RS21764 (March 9). Washington: Congressional Research Service.

Lopez, Vanessa. 2012. Venezuelan Assistance to Cuba. *Focus on Cuba,* no. 155 (January 10). Institute for Cuban and Cuban-American Studies, University of Miami. Available at http://ctp.iccas.miami.edu/FOCUS_Web/Issue155.htm.

Luis, Luis R. 2009. Cuban External Finance and the Global Economic Crisis. *Cuba in Transition* 19: 108–15. Papers and Proceedings of the Nineteenth Annual Meeting. Miami: Association for the Study of the Cuban Economy.

Luis, Luis R. 2012. Cuba: External Cash Flow, Barter Trade and Potential Shocks. *Cuba in Transition* 22: 102–10. Papers and Proceedings of the Twenty-Second Annual Meeting. Miami: Association for the Study of the Cuban Economy.

Lum, Thomas, Hannah Fischer, Julissa Gomez-Granger, and Anne Leland. 2009. *China's Foreign Aid Activities in Africa, Latin America, and Southeast Asia*. CRS Report to Congress R40361 (February 25). Washington: Congressional Research Service.

Maskus, Keith E. 2012. *Private Rights and Public Problems: The Global Economics of Intellectual Property in the 21st Century*. Washington: Peterson Institute for International Economics.

Mesa-Lago, Carmelo. 2009. The Cuban Economy in 2008–2009. Unpublished paper. Available at http://stonecenter.tulane.edu/uploads/Mesa-Lago-1305235386.pdf.

Mesa-Lago, Carmelo. 2011. Social Services in Cuba: Antecedents, Quality, Financial Sustainability and Policies for the Future. In *The Cuban Economy: Recent Trends*, ed. José Raúl Perales. Washington: Woodrow Wilson Center.

Moody's Investor Service. 2011. Moody's Disclosures on Credit Ratings of Cuba, Government of (December 23). Available at www.moodys.com/research/Moodys-Disclosures-on-Credit-Ratings-of-Cuba-Government-of--PR_233920.

Mora, Frank. 2006. Young Blood: Continuity and Change within Cuba's Revolutionary Armed Forces. *Hemisphere* 17 (Fall). Cuba Research Institute. Available at http://cri.fiu.edu/research/hemisphere-magazine/hemisphere-volume-17.pdf.

Morales, Emilio. 2013. *The U.S. Is Second Leading Country of Tourists in Cuba* (January 28). Havana Consulting Group LLC. Available at http://thehavanaconsultinggroups.com/index.php?option=com_content&view=article&id=340%3Athe-us-is-second-leading-country-of-tourists-in-cuba&catid=36%3Atourism-&lang=en.

Morales, Emilio, and Joseph L. Scarpaci. 2012. *Opening up on both shorelines helps increase remittances sent to Cuba in 2011 by about 20%.* Havana Consulting Group LLC. Available at www.thehavanaconsultinggroup.com/index.php?option=com_content&view=article&id=324%3Aopening-up-on-both-shorelines-helps-increase-remittances-sent-to-cuba-in-2011-by-about-20-&catid=48%3Aremittances&lang=en (accessed on May 2, 2013).

Morales, Emilio, and Joseph L. Scarpaci. 2013. *Remittances Drive the Cuban Economy* (June 11). Havana Consulting Group LLC. Available at http://thehavanaconsultinggroups.com/index.php?option=com_content&view=article&id=345%3Aremittances-drive-the-cuban-economy&catid=48%3Aremittances&lang=en.

Motel, Seth, and Eileen Patten. 2012. *Hispanics of Cuban Origin in the United States.* Hispanic Trends Project (June 27). Washington: Pew Research Center. Available at www.pewhispanic.org/2012/06/27/hispanics-of-cuban-origin-in-the-united-states-2010 (accessed on March 4, 2013).

Nerurkar, Neelesh, and Mark P. Sullivan. 2011. *Cuba's Offshore Oil Development: Background and US Policy Consideration.* CRS Report to Congress R41522 (November 28). Washington: Congressional Service Research.

Orozco, Manuel. 2009. On Remittances, Markets and the Law: The Cuban Experience in Recent Times. *Cuba in Transition* 19: 406–11. Papers and Proceedings of the Nineteenth Annual Meeting. Miami: Association for the Study of the Cuban Economy.

Orozco, Manuel. 2012. *The Market for Money Transfers: Ranking of Remittance Service Providers in Latin America and the Caribbean.* Available at www.thedialogue.org/uploads/Remittances_and_Development/LatAm_Final_120712.pdf.

Ortiz, José A. 2000. The Illegal Expropriation of Property in Cuba: A Historical and Legal Analysis of the Taking and a Survey of Restitution Schemes for a Post-Socialist Cuba. *Loyola of Los Angeles International and Comparative Law Review* 22, no. 3: 321–55.

Paris Club. 2013. The Paris Club Releases Comprehensive Data on Its Claims as of 31 December 2012. Press release, May 29. Available at www.clubdeparis.org/sections/donnees-chiffrees/encours-du-club-paris_1/downloadFile/attachedFile_4_f0/2012a.pdf?nocache=1369818219.53.

Patiño, Christian Santiago. 2009. The Cuban Sugar Dilemma: The Prospect for a Green Future. *Cuba in Transition* 15: 299–308. Papers and Proceedings of the Fifteenth Annual Meeting. Miami: Association for the Study of the Cuban Economy.

Perales, Jóse Raúl, ed. 2010. *The United States and Cuba: Implications of an Economic Relationship.* Latin American Program (August). Washington: Woodrow Wilson International Center. Available at www.wilsoncenter.org/sites/default/files/LAP_Cuba_Implications.pdf.

Pérez, Lorenzo. 2008. Cuba: Access to Capital Markets, External Debt Burden, and Debt Relief. *Cuba in Transition* 18: 160–67. Papers and Proceedings of the Eighteenth Annual Meeting. Miami: Association for the Study of the Cuban Economy.

Pérez-López, Jorge, and Carmelo Mesa-Lago. 2009. Cuban GDP Statistics under the Special Period: Discontinuities, Obfuscation, and Puzzles. *Cuba in Transition* 19: 153–67. Papers and Proceedings of the Nineteenth Annual Meeting. Miami: Association for the Study of the Cuban Economy.

Pérez-López, Jorge F., and Matias F. Travieso-Diaz. 2001. The Contribution of BITs to Cuba's Foreign Investment Program. *Law and Policy in International Business* 32, no. 3 (Spring): 529–71.

Pérez, Villanueva, Omar Everleny. 2012. The Cuban Economy: An Evaluation and Proposals for Necessary Policy Changes. In *Cuban Economic and Social Development*, ed. Jorge Domínguez, Omar Everleny Pérez Villanueva, Mayra Espina Prieto, and Lorena Barberia. Cambridge, MA: Harvard University Press.

Pérez, Villanueva, Omar Everleny, and Pavel Vidal Alejandro. 2012. La Inversión Extranjera Directa y la Actualización del Modelo Económico Cubano [Foreign Direct Investment and Updating Cuba's Economic Model]. Presentation to the annual conference of the Center for the Study for the Cuban Economy (CEEC), June.

Perry, Joseph M., Louis A. Woods, and Stephen L. Shapiro. 2000. Intellectual Property Rights and International Trade in Cuban Products. *Cuba in Transition* 11: 77–87. Papers and Proceedings of the Eleventh Annual Meeting. Miami: Association for the Study of the Cuban Economy.

Peters, Philip. 2006. *Cuba's Small Entrepreneurs: Down but Not Out* (September). Arlington, VA: Lexington Institute. Available at www.lexingtoninstitute.org/library/resources/documents/Cuba/ResearchProducts/cubas_small_entrepreneurs.pdf.

Potestà, Michele. 2012. Republic of Italy v. Republic of Cuba. *American Journal of International Law* 106, no. 2 (April): 341–47.

Powell, H. Jefferson. 1999. The Founders and the President's Authority over Foreign Affairs. *William and Mary Law Review* 40, no. 5 (May).

Pöyhönen, Pentti. 1963. A Tentative Model for the Volume of Trade between Countries. *Weltwirtschaftliches Archiv* 90, no. 1: 93–100.

Pregelj, Vladimir N. 2005. *Normal-Trade Relations (Most-Favored-Nation) Policy of the United States.* CRS Report to Congress RL31558 (December 15). Washington: Congressional Research Service.

Prislan, Vid, and Ruben Zandvliet. 2013. Labor Provisions in Bilateral Investment Treaties: Does the New US Model BIT Provide a Template for the Future? *Columbia FDI Perspectives*, no. 92 (April 1). Available at www.vcc.columbia.edu/content/labor-provisions-bilateral-investment-treaties-does-new-us-model-bit-provide-template-future.

Propst, Stephen F. 2011. *Presidential Authority to Modify Economic Sanctions Against Cuba.* Washington: Hogan Lovells.

Reid-Henry, S. M. 2010. *The Cuban Cure: Reason and Resistance in Global Science.* Chicago: University of Chicago Press.

Ritter, Archibald R. M. 1990. The Cuban Economy in the 1990s: External Challenges and Policy Imperatives. *Journal of Interamerican Studies and World Affairs* 32, no. 3 (Autumn): 117–49.

Ritter, Archibald R. M. 2005. *Cuba's Underground Economy.* Carleton Economic Papers. Carleton University, Department of Economics.

Rose, Andrew K. 2004. Do We Really Know that the WTO Increases Trade? *American Economic Review* 94, no. 1 (March): 98–114.

Sanchelima, Jesus. 2002. Selected Aspects of Cuba's Intellectual Property Laws. *Cuba in Transition* 15: 213–19. Papers and Proceedings of the Fifteenth Annual Meeting. Miami: Association for the Study of the Cuban Economy.

Schenk, Christopher J. 2010. *Geologic Assessment of Undiscovered Oil and Gas Resources of the North Cuba Basin, Cuba.* Cuba: U.S. Geological Survey Open-File Report 2010–1029. Available at http://pubs.usgs.gov/of/2010/1029.

Selden, Zachary A. 1999. *Economic Sanctions as Instruments of American Foreign Policy.* Westport: Praeger.

Sotolongo, María Lourdes Ruíz. 2011. Business Brief: Cuba. *World Intellectual Property Review* (January 1). Available at www.worldipreview.com (accessed on April 23, 2013).

Suchlicki, Jaime. 2007. Challenges to a Post-Castro Cuba. *Harvard International Review.* Available at http://hir.harvard.edu/challenges-to-a-post-castro-cuba.

Sullivan, Mark. 2011. *Cuba: Issues for the 111th Congress.* CRS Report to Congress R40193 (January 4). Washington: Congressional Research Service.

Sullivan, Mark. 2012a. *Cuba: U.S. Restrictions on Travel and Remittances.* CRS Report to Congress RL31139 (November 9). Washington: Congressional Research Service.

Sullivan, Mark. 2012b. *Cuba Issues for 112th Congress*. CRS Report to Congress R41617 (November 6). Washington: Congressional Research Service.

Sullivan, Mark. 2013. *Cuba: U.S. Policy and Issues for the 113th Congress*. CRS Report to Congress R43024 (June 12). Washington: Congressional Research Service.

Tinbergen, Jan. 1962. An Analysis of World Trade Flows. In *Shaping the World Economy*, ed. Jan Tinbergen. New York: Twentieth Century Fund.

Travieso-Díaz, Matías F. 1997. *The Laws and Legal System of a Free-Market Cuba: A Prospectus for Business*. Westport, CT: Quorum Books.

Travieso-Díaz, Matías F. 2002. Alternative Recommendations for Dealing with Expropriated U.S. Property in Post-Castro Cuba. *Cuba in Transition* 12: 101–15. Papers and Proceedings of the Twelfth Annual Meeting. Miami: Association for the Study of the Cuban Economy.

Tuininga, Kevin. 2008. International Commercial Arbitration in Cuba. *Emory International Law Review* 22: 572–625. Available at www.law.emory.edu.

UNCTAD (United Nations Conference on Trade and Development). 2012. *World Investment Report 2012*. New York and Geneva: United Nations.

US Department of Commerce. 2011. *Profile of U.S. Resident Travelers Visiting Overseas Destinations: 2011 Outbound*. Office of Tourism and Travel Industries. Washington. Available at http://travel.trade.gov/outreachpages/download_data_table/2011_Outbound_Profile.pdf.

USITC (United States International Trade Commission). 2001. *The Economic Impact of U.S. Sanctions with Respect to Cuba*. USITC Publication 3398 (February). Washington.

USITC (United States International Trade Commission). 2007. *U.S. Agricultural Sales to Cuba: Certain Economic Effects of U.S. Restrictions*. Investigation No. 332-489. USITC Publication 3932 (July). Washington. Available at www.usitc.gov/publications/332/pub3932.pdf.

USTR (United States Trade Representative). 2004. *The Dominican Republic-Central America-United States Free Trade Agreement*. Washington. Available at www.ustr.gov/trade-agreements/free-trade-agreements/cafta-dr-dominican-republic-central-america-fta/final-text.

USTR (United States Trade Representative). 2007. *Trade Capacity Building Success Stories: Dominican Republic-Central America-United States Free Trade Agreement (CAFTA-DR)*. USTR Policy Brief. Washington.

USTR (United States Trade Representative). 2011. *Ninth Report to Congress on the Operation of the Caribbean Basin Economic Recovery* Act (December 31). Washington. Available at www.ustr.gov/webfm_send/3214.

USTR (United States Trade Representative). 2012. Bilateral and Regional Negotiations and Agreements. In *2012 Trade Policy Agenda and 2011 Annual Report*. Washington. Available at www.ustr.gov/sites/default/files/Chapter%20III.%20Bilateral%20and%20Regional%20Negotiations%20and%20Agreements.pdf.

Wasem, Ruth Ellen. 2009. *Cuban Migration to the United States: Policy and Trends*. CRS Report to Congress R40566. Washington: Congressional Research Service.

Wasem, Ruth Ellen. 2012. *U.S. Immigration Policy on Permanent Admissions*. CRS Report to Congress RL32235. Washington: Congressional Research Service.

WIPO (World Intellectual Property Organization). 2004. Intellectual Property as a Lever for Economic Growth: The Latin American and Caribbean Experience–Part II. *WIPO Magazine*, no. 2 (March/April): 2–6. Available at www.wipo.int/export/sites/www/wipo_magazine/en/pdf/2004/wipo_pub_121_2004_03-04.pdf.

WIPO (World Intellectual Property Organization). 2011. *Summaries of Conventions, Treaties and Agreements Administered by WIPO*. Publication no. 442E/11. Available at www.wipo.int.

Zuo, Pin. 2010. A Survey of the Relationship between Cuba and China: A Chinese Perspective. *Cuba in Transition* 20: 193–299. Papers and Proceedings of the Twentieth Annual Meeting. Miami: Association for the Study of the Cuban Economy.

Index

Other Publications from the
Peterson Institute for International Economics

WORKING PAPERS

* = out of print

POLICY ANALYSES IN INTERNATIONAL ECONOMICS Series

Toward Renewed Economic Growth in Latin America* Bela Balassa, Gerardo M. Bueno, Pedro Pablo Kuczynski, and Mario Henrique Simonsen
1986 ISBN 0-88132-045-5
Capital Flight and Third World Debt*
Donald R. Lessard and John Williamson, eds.
1987 ISBN 0-88132-053-6
The Canada-United States Free Trade Agreement: The Global Impact* Jeffrey J. Schott and Murray G. Smith, eds.
1988 ISBN 0-88132-073-0
World Agricultural Trade: Building a Consensus* William M. Miner and Dale E. Hathaway, eds.
1988 ISBN 0-88132-071-3
Japan in the World Economy* Bela Balassa and Marcus Noland
1988 ISBN 0-88132-041-2
America in the World Economy: A Strategy for the 1990s* C. Fred Bergsten
1988 ISBN 0-88132-089-7
Managing the Dollar: From the Plaza to the Louvre* Yoichi Funabashi
1988, 2d ed. 1989 ISBN 0-88132-097-8
United States External Adjustment and the World Economy* William R. Cline
May 1989 ISBN 0-88132-048-X
Free Trade Areas and U.S. Trade Policy*
Jeffrey J. Schott, ed.
May 1989 ISBN 0-88132-094-3
Dollar Politics: Exchange Rate Policymaking in the United States* I. M. Destler and C. Randall Henning
September 1989 ISBN 0-88132-079-X
Latin American Adjustment: How Much Has Happened?* John Williamson, ed.
April 1990 ISBN 0-88132-125-7
The Future of World Trade in Textiles and Apparel* William R. Cline
1987, 2d ed. June 1999 ISBN 0-88132-110-9
Completing the Uruguay Round: A Results-Oriented Approach to the GATT Trade Negotiations* Jeffrey J. Schott, ed.
September 1990 ISBN 0-88132-130-3
Economic Sanctions Reconsidered (2 volumes)
Economic Sanctions Reconsidered:
Supplemental Case Histories
Gary Clyde Hufbauer, Jeffrey J. Schott, and Kimberly Ann Elliott
1985, 2d ed. Dec. 1990 ISBN cloth 0-88132-115-X
ISBN paper 0-88132-105-2
Economic Sanctions Reconsidered: History and Current Policy Gary C. Hufbauer, Jeffrey J. Schott, and Kimberly Ann Elliott
December 1990 ISBN cloth 0-88132-140-0
ISBN paper 0-88132-136-2
Pacific Basin Developing Countries: Prospects for the Future* Marcus Noland
January 1991 ISBN cloth 0-88132-141-9
ISBN paper 0-88132-081-1
Currency Convertibility in Eastern Europe*
John Williamson, ed.
October 1991 ISBN 0-88132-128-1

International Adjustment and Financing: The Lessons of 1985-1991* C. Fred Bergsten, ed.
January 1992 ISBN 0-88132-112-5
North American Free Trade: Issues and Recommendations* Gary Clyde Hufbauer and Jeffrey J. Schott
April 1992 ISBN 0-88132-120-6
Narrowing the U.S. Current Account Deficit*
Alan J. Lenz
June 1992 ISBN 0-88132-103-6
The Economics of Global Warming
William R. Cline
June 1992 ISBN 0-88132-132-X
US Taxation of International Income: Blueprint for Reform Gary Clyde Hufbauer, assisted by Joanna M. van Rooij
October 1992 ISBN 0-88132-134-6
Who's Bashing Whom? Trade Conflict in High-Technology Industries Laura D'Andrea Tyson
November 1992 ISBN 0-88132-106-0
Korea in the World Economy* Il SaKong
January 1993 ISBN 0-88132-183-4
Pacific Dynamism and the International Economic System* C. Fred Bergsten and Marcus Noland, eds.
May 1993 ISBN 0-88132-196-6
Economic Consequences of Soviet Disintegration* John Williamson, ed.
May 1993 ISBN 0-88132-190-7
Reconcilable Differences? United States-Japan Economic Conflict* C. Fred Bergsten and Marcus Noland
June 1993 ISBN 0-88132-129-X
Does Foreign Exchange Intervention Work?
Kathryn M. Dominguez and Jeffrey A. Frankel
September 1993 ISBN 0-88132-104-4
Sizing Up U.S. Export Disincentives*
J. David Richardson
September 1993 ISBN 0-88132-107-9
NAFTA: An Assessment Gary Clyde Hufbauer and Jeffrey J. Schott, *rev. ed.*
October 1993 ISBN 0-88132-199-0
Adjusting to Volatile Energy Prices
Philip K. Verleger, Jr.
November 1993 ISBN 0-88132-069-2
The Political Economy of Policy Reform
John Williamson, ed.
January 1994 ISBN 0-88132-195-8
Measuring the Costs of Protection in the United States Gary Clyde Hufbauer and Kimberly Ann Elliott
January 1994 ISBN 0-88132-108-7
The Dynamics of Korean Economic Development* Cho Soon
March 1994 ISBN 0-88132-162-1
Reviving the European Union*
C. Randall Henning, Eduard Hochreiter, and Gary Clyde Hufbauer, eds.
April 1994 ISBN 0-88132-208-3
China in the World Economy Nicholas R. Lardy
April 1994 ISBN 0-88132-200-8
Greening the GATT: Trade, Environment, and the Future Daniel C. Esty
July 1994 ISBN 0-88132-205-9

Safeguarding Prosperity in a Global Financial System: The Future International Financial Architecture, Independent Task Force Report Sponsored by the Council on Foreign Relations
Morris Goldstein, Project Director
October 1999 ISBN 0-88132-287-3

Avoiding the Apocalypse: The Future of the Two Koreas Marcus Noland
June 2000 ISBN 0-88132-278-4

Assessing Financial Vulnerability: An Early Warning System for Emerging Markets
Morris Goldstein, Graciela Kaminsky, and Carmen Reinhart
June 2000 ISBN 0-88132-237-7

Global Electronic Commerce: A Policy Primer
Catherine L. Mann, Sue E. Eckert, and Sarah Cleeland Knight
July 2000 ISBN 0-88132-274-1

The WTO after Seattle Jeffrey J. Schott, ed.
July 2000 ISBN 0-88132-290-3

Intellectual Property Rights in the Global Economy Keith E. Maskus
August 2000 ISBN 0-88132-282-2

The Political Economy of the Asian Financial Crisis Stephan Haggard
August 2000 ISBN 0-88132-283-0

Transforming Foreign Aid: United States Assistance in the 21st Century Carol Lancaster
August 2000 ISBN 0-88132-291-1

Fighting the Wrong Enemy: Antiglobal Activists and Multinational Enterprises
Edward M. Graham
September 2000 ISBN 0-88132-272-5

Globalization and the Perceptions of American Workers Kenneth Scheve and Matthew J. Slaughter
March 2001 ISBN 0-88132-295-4

World Capital Markets: Challenge to the G-10
Wendy Dobson and Gary Clyde Hufbauer, assisted by Hyun Koo Cho
May 2001 ISBN 0-88132-301-2

Prospects for Free Trade in the Americas
Jeffrey J. Schott
August 2001 ISBN 0-88132-275-X

Toward a North American Community: Lessons from the Old World for the New
Robert A. Pastor
August 2001 ISBN 0-88132-328-4

Measuring the Costs of Protection in Europe: European Commercial Policy in the 2000s
Patrick A. Messerlin
September 2001 ISBN 0-88132-273-3

Job Loss from Imports: Measuring the Costs
Lori G. Kletzer
September 2001 ISBN 0-88132-296-2

No More Bashing: Building a New Japan–United States Economic Relationship C. Fred Bergsten, Takatoshi Ito, and Marcus Noland
October 2001 ISBN 0-88132-286-5

Why Global Commitment Really Matters!
Howard Lewis III and J. David Richardson
October 2001 ISBN 0-88132-298-9

Leadership Selection in the Major Multilaterals
Miles Kahler
November 2001 ISBN 0-88132-335-7

The International Financial Architecture: What's New? What's Missing? Peter B. Kenen
November 2001 ISBN 0-88132-297-0

Delivering on Debt Relief: From IMF Gold to a New Aid Architecture John Williamson and Nancy Birdsall, with Brian Deese
April 2002 ISBN 0-88132-331-4

Imagine There's No Country: Poverty, Inequality, and Growth in the Era of Globalization Surjit S. Bhalla
September 2002 ISBN 0-88132-348-9

Reforming Korea's Industrial Conglomerates
Edward M. Graham
January 2003 ISBN 0-88132-337-3

Industrial Policy in an Era of Globalization: Lessons from Asia Marcus Noland and Howard Pack
March 2003 ISBN 0-88132-350-0

Reintegrating India with the World Economy
T. N. Srinivasan and Suresh D. Tendulkar
March 2003 ISBN 0-88132-280-6

After the Washington Consensus: Restarting Growth and Reform in Latin America Pedro-Pablo Kuczynski and John Williamson, eds.
March 2003 ISBN 0-88132-347-0

The Decline of US Labor Unions and the Role of Trade Robert E. Baldwin
June 2003 ISBN 0-88132-341-1

Can Labor Standards Improve under Globalization? Kimberly Ann Elliott and Richard B. Freeman
June 2003 ISBN 0-88132-332-2

Crimes and Punishments? Retaliation under the WTO Robert Z. Lawrence
October 2003 ISBN 0-88132-359-4

Inflation Targeting in the World Economy
Edwin M. Truman
October 2003 ISBN 0-88132-345-4

Foreign Direct Investment and Tax Competition
John H. Mutti
November 2003 ISBN 0-88132-352-7

Has Globalization Gone Far Enough? The Costs of Fragmented Markets Scott C. Bradford and Robert Z. Lawrence
February 2004 ISBN 0-88132-349-7

Food Regulation and Trade: Toward a Safe and Open Global System Tim Josling, Donna Roberts, and David Orden
March 2004 ISBN 0-88132-346-2

Controlling Currency Mismatches in Emerging Markets Morris Goldstein and Philip Turner
April 2004 ISBN 0-88132-360-8

Free Trade Agreements: US Strategies and Priorities Jeffrey J. Schott, ed.
April 2004 ISBN 0-88132-361-6

Trade Policy and Global Poverty
William R. Cline
June 2004 ISBN 0-88132-365-9

Bailouts or Bail-ins? Responding to Financial Crises in Emerging Economies Nouriel Roubini and Brad Setser
August 2004 ISBN 0-88132-371-3

Transforming the European Economy Martin Neil Baily and Jacob Funk Kirkegaard
September 2004 ISBN 0-88132-343-8

Foreign Direct Investment and Development: Launching a Second Generation of Policy Research, Avoiding the Mistakes of the First, Reevaluating Policies for Developed and Developing Countries   Theodore H. Moran
April 2011   ISBN 978-0-88132-600-0
How Latvia Came through the Financial Crisis
Anders Åslund and Valdis Dombrovskis
May 2011   ISBN 978-0-88132-602-4
Global Trade in Services: Fear, Facts, and Offshoring   J. Bradford Jensen
August 2011   ISBN 978-0-88132-601-7
NAFTA and Climate Change Meera Fickling and Jeffrey J. Schott
September 2011   ISBN 978-0-88132-436-5
Eclipse: Living in the Shadow of China's Economic Dominance   Arvind Subramanian
September 2011   ISBN 978-0-88132-606-2
Flexible Exchange Rates for a Stable World Economy   Joseph E. Gagnon with Marc Hinterschweiger
September 2011   ISBN 978-0-88132-627-7
The Arab Economies in a Changing World, 2d ed.   Marcus Noland and Howard Pack
November 2011   ISBN 978-0-88132-628-4
Sustaining China's Economic Growth After the Global Financial Crisis   Nicholas R. Lardy
January 2012   ISBN 978-0-88132-626-0
Who Needs to Open the Capital Account?
Olivier Jeanne, Arvind Subramanian, and John Williamson
April 2012   ISBN 978-0-88132-511-9
Devaluing to Prosperity: Misaligned Currencies and Their Growth Consequences Surjit S. Bhalla
August 2012   ISBN 978-0-88132-623-9
Private Rights and Public Problems: The Global Economics of Intellectual Property in the 21st Century   Keith E. Maskus
September 2012   ISBN 978-0-88132-507-2
Global Economics in Extraordinary Times: Essays in Honor of John Williamson
C. Fred Bergsten and C. Randall Henning, eds.
November 2012   ISBN 978-0-88132-662-8
Rising Tide: Is Growth in Emerging Economies Good for the United States?   Lawrence Edwards and Robert Z. Lawrence
February 2013   ISBN 978-0-88132-500-3
Responding to Financial Crisis: Lessons from Asia Then, the United States and Europe Now
Changyong Rhee and Adam S. Posen, eds
October 2013   ISBN 978-0-88132-674-1
Fueling Up: The Economic Implications of America's Oil and Gas Boom
Trevor Houser and Shashank Mohan
January 2014   ISBN 978-0-88132-656-7
How Latin America Weathered the Global Financial Crisis   José De Gregorio
January 2014   ISBN 978-0-88132-678-9

SPECIAL REPORTS

1   Promoting World Recovery: A Statement on Global Economic Strategy*
by 26 Economists from Fourteen Countries
December 1982   ISBN 0-88132-013-7

2   Prospects for Adjustment in Argentina, Brazil, and Mexico: Responding to the Debt Crisis*   John Williamson, ed.
June 1983   ISBN 0-88132-016-1
3   Inflation and Indexation: Argentina, Brazil, and Israel*   John Williamson, ed.
March 1985   ISBN 0-88132-037-4
4   Global Economic Imb alances*
C. Fred Bergsten, ed.
March 1986   ISBN 0-88132-042-0
5   African Debt and Financing*   Carol Lancaster and John Williamson, eds.
May 1986   ISBN 0-88132-044-7
6   Resolving the Global Economic Crisis: After Wall Street*   by Thirty-three Economists from Thirteen Countries
December 1987   ISBN 0-88132-070-6
7   World Economic Problems*   Kimberly Ann Elliott and John Williamson, eds.
April 1988   ISBN 0-88132-055-2
Reforming World Agricultural Trade*
by Twenty-nine Professionals from Seventeen Countries
1988   ISBN 0-88132-088-9
8   Economic Relations Between the United States and Korea: Conflict or Cooperation?*
Thomas O. Bayard and Soogil Young, eds.
January 1989   ISBN 0-88132-068-4
9   Whither APEC? The Progress to Date and Agenda for the Future* C. Fred Bergsten, ed.
October 1997   ISBN 0-88132-248-2
10   Economic Integration of the Korean Peninsula   Marcus Noland, ed.
January 1998   ISBN 0-88132-255-5
11   Restarting Fast Track*   Jeffrey J. Schott, ed.
April 1998   ISBN 0-88132-259-8
12   Launching New Global Trade Talks: An Action Agenda   Jeffrey J. Schott, ed.
September 1998   ISBN 0-88132-266-0
13   Japan's Financial Crisis and Its Parallels to US Experience   Ryoichi Mikitani and Adam S. Posen, eds.
September 2000   ISBN 0-88132-289-X
14   The Ex-Im Bank in the 21st Century: A New Approach   Gary Clyde Hufbauer and Rita M. Rodriguez, eds.
January 2001   ISBN 0-88132-300-4
15   The Korean Diaspora in the World Economy   C. Fred Bergsten and Inbom Choi, eds.
January 2003   ISBN 0-88132-358-6
16   Dollar Overvaluation and the World Economy   C. Fred Bergsten and John Williamson, eds.
February 2003   ISBN 0-88132-351-9
17   Dollar Adjustment: How Far? Against What?   C. Fred Bergsten and John Williamson, eds.
November 2004   ISBN 0-88132-378-0
18   The Euro at Five: Ready for a Global Role?
Adam S. Posen, ed.
April 2005   ISBN 0-88132-380-2
19   Reforming the IMF for the 21st Century
Edwin M. Truman, ed.

WORKS IN PROGRESS

**Confronting the Curse: The Economics and
Geopolitics of Natural Resource Governance**
Marcus Noland and Cullen S. Hendrix
**Markets over Mao: The Rise of the Private
Sector in China**   Nicholas R. Lardy
Inside the Euro Crisis: An Eyewitness Account
Simeon Djankov
Managing the Euro Area Debt Crisis
William R. Cline
**From Wariness to Partnership: Integrating the
Economies of India and the United States**
C. Fred Bergsten and Arvind Subramanian
**Bridging the Pacific: Toward Free Trade and
Investment Between China and the United
States**   C. Fred Bergsten and
Gary Clyde Hufbauer

DISTRIBUTORS OUTSIDE THE UNITED STATES

Australia, New Zealand,
and Papua New Guinea
Co Info Pty Ltd
648 Whitehorse Road Mitcham VIC 3132
Australia
Tel: +61 3 9210 77567
Fax: +61 3 9210 7788
Email: babadilla@coinfo.com.au
www.coinfo.com.au

India, Bangladesh, Nepal, and Sri Lanka
Viva Books Private Limited
Mr. Vinod Vasishtha
4737/23 Ansari Road
Daryaganj, New Delhi 110002
India
Tel: 91-11-4224-2200
Fax: 91-11-4224-2240
Email: viva@vivagroupindia.net
www.vivagroupindia.com

Mexico, Central America, South America,
and Puerto Rico
US PubRep, Inc.
311 Dean Drive
Rockville, MD 20851
Tel: 301-838-9276
Fax: 301-838-9278
Email: c.falk@ieee.org

Asia *(Brunei, Burma, Cambodia, China,*
Hong Kong, Indonesia, Korea, Laos, Malaysia,
Philippines, Singapore, Taiwan, Thailand,
and Vietnam)
East-West Export Books (EWEB)
University of Hawaii Press
2840 Kolowalu Street
Honolulu, Hawaii 96822-1888
Tel: 808-956-8830
Fax: 808-988-6052
Email: eweb@hawaii.edu

Canada
Renouf Bookstore
5369 Canotek Road, Unit 1
Ottawa, Ontario KlJ 9J3, Canada
Tel: 613-745-2665
Fax: 613-745-7660
www.renoufbooks.com

Japan
United Publishers Services Ltd.
1-32-5, Higashi-shinagawa
Shinagawa-ku, Tokyo 140-0002
Japan
Tel: 81-3-5479-7251
Fax: 81-3-5479-7307
Email: purchasing@ups.co.jp
For trade accounts only. Individuals will find
Institute books in leading Tokyo bookstores.

Middle East
MERIC
2 Bahgat Ali Street, El Masry Towers
Tower D, Apt. 24
Zamalek, Cairo
Egypt
Tel. 20-2-7633824
Fax: 20-2-7369355
Email: mahmoud_fouda@mericonline.com
www.mericonline.com

United Kingdom, Europe
(including Russia and Turkey), **Africa,**
and Israel
The Eurospan Group
c/o Turpin Distribution
Pegasus Drive
Stratton Business Park
Biggleswade, Bedfordshire
SG18 8TQ
United Kingdom
Tel: 44 (0) 1767-604972
Fax: 44 (0) 1767-601640
Email: eurospan@turpin-distribution.com
www.eurospangroup.com/bookstore

Visit our website at:
www.piie.com
E-mail orders to:
petersonmail@presswarehouse.com